Direct Selling POWER

Expert advice to accelerate your business

PowerDynamics PUBLISHING

𝒫ower𝒟ynamics
PUBLISHING

PowerDynamics Publishing
San Francisco, California
www.powerdynamicspub.com

ISBN: 978-0-9644906-6-6

Library of Congress Control Number: 2010921292

Printed in the United States of America.

This book is printed on acid-free paper.

For you:

We dedicate this book to you, the direct seller, whether you are experienced or just getting started, who recognizes the power of knowing what to do and when to do it to have a wildly successful direct selling career. We salute you for embracing knowledge to advance your career—and we celebrate your commitment to being the best you can be!

The Co-authors of Direct Selling Power

Table of Contents

Acknowledgments

Gratitude is an important part of being a successful direct seller. We are truly grateful that you have embraced our ideas and are granting us the opportunity to make a contribution to you. Before we share our wisdom and experience with you, we have a few people to thank for turning our vision for this book into a reality.

This book is the bright concept of Caterina Rando, the founder of PowerDynamics Publishing and a respected direct sales coach and keynote speaker with whom many direct sellers have worked to grow their businesses. Working closely with many direct sales professionals, direct selling companies and the Direct Selling Women's Alliance, she realized the need for a gathering of top experts with information to enhance the career of direct sellers. The result was putting our best ideas into this comprehensive book.

Without Caterina's "take action" spirit, her positive attitude and her commitment to excellence, you would not be reading this wonderful book, of which we are all so proud.

We also want to thank Nicki Keohohou, Grace Keohohou and the entire Direct Selling Women's Alliance team, for their partnership on this project. As DSWA-approved speakers and trainers, we are so grateful for what this organization does for women (and men) in the direct selling profession. We are proud of our involvement with the DSWA and our collaboration on this project.

Additionally, all of our efforts were supported by a truly dedicated group of people that make up our publication team. They worked diligently with a commitment to put together the best possible book for you. We are truly grateful for everyone's stellar contribution.

To Ruth Schwartz, project manager and copyeditor extraordinaire, who brought her many years of publishing and direct selling experience to this project. The wisdom, professional expertise, guidance and support she provided to everyone on the team and to all of the co-authors is deeply appreciated.

To Laura Piester, who was key to bringing us together to participate in this amazing publication. We appreciate your passion for direct selling, your follow through and your positive "make it happen" attitude.

To Tammy Tribble, who brought her creative talent to the cover design and book layout, thank you for your enthusiasm, joyful nature, problem-solving and attention to detail throughout this project.

To Bernie Burson, who provided us with a keen eye and an elegant sense for what is on every page, thank you for your support, expertise and contribution.

We also acknowledge each other for delivering outstanding information, guidance and advice. Through our work on this book and with our clients, we are truly committed to enhancing the careers of direct selling professionals. We are truly grateful that we get to do work that we love and make a contribution to so many in the process. We do not take our good fortune lightly. We are clear in our mission—to make a genuine contribution to you, the reader. Thank you for granting us this extraordinary opportunity.

The Co-authors of Direct Selling Power

Introduction

Congratulations! You have opened an incredible resource, packed with great ideas that will enhance your career in ways you cannot yet imagine. You are about to discover the exquisite magic of *Direct Selling Power.*

Your direct selling success comes as the result of more than talent, commitment and hard work. Your career success will also be determined by how you improve your business skills in booking, selling, recruiting and leading your team, as well as your personal skills in communications, accountability and responsibility. In fact, your success is determined by *all* that you say and do as you build your business. We know you want to be the absolute best you can be.

With this book, you can quickly learn how leaders in direct selling conduct themselves to get the very best results. As top experts in each of our respective specialties, we've joined together to give you the most powerful direct selling information and strategies available.

Each of us has seen how even small changes in behavior and daily actions can transform and uplift your career. We have so much to share with you, including:
- Knowing how to manage your life and have a successful direct selling business at the same time.
- Learning how to effectively communicate and listen as you build your team

- Knowing how to efficiently book, sell, recruit and follow-up
- Learn how to use public speaking to grow your business

All the direct selling experts you will meet in this book want you to build your business in the best possible way. We have outlined for you our top tips and included the most expert advice we have to advance your career.

To get the most out of *Direct Selling Power*, we recommend that you read through it once, cover to cover. Then go back and follow the advice that applies to you, in the chapters most relevant to your current situation. Every improvement you make will make a difference in your confidence and effectiveness and will impact the growth of your business and your team.

We encourage you to use the information in these pages on your team calls and at your monthly meetings. Use *Direct Selling Power* as a study guide with your team. There is a huge amount of value here for your whole team. Be sure to use it.

Know that just learning what to do will not transform your direct selling career. You must *take action* and apply the strategies, tips and tactics we share in these pages. Apply the many skills in this book and you will reap many rewards. With our knowledge and your action, we are confident that, like our thousands of satisfied clients, you too will master the magic of *Direct Selling Power*.

To your unlimited success!

The Co-authors of Direct Selling Power

The Power of Direct Selling
Leading the Way for Entrepreneurs

By Nicki Keohohou

You are reading this because you are either looking at entering the world of direct selling or have already taken steps toward an amazing life as an entrepreneur. Congratulations!

This profession is one of the most empowering career choices you can pursue. Today, more than ever, direct selling is leading the way for those of you who want to take control of your destiny. I am proud of our profession and hope to instill a clear understanding of why direct selling is the greatest career you can pursue.

What is Direct Selling?
The Direct Selling Women's Alliance brings together the hearts, minds, and wisdom of distributors that participate in party plan, person-to-person sales and network marketing businesses to create a unified profession.

There is some confusion about what the term direct selling means, even within our own industry. To clear things up, the DSWA has created this simple diagram that explains the three methods of marketing under the term "Direct Selling."

Party Plan	Person-to-Person	Network Marketing (MLM)
Shared emphasis on product sales and team building	Emphasis on product sales and services	Strong emphasis on building a team
Products sold primarily through in-home shows	Products and services sold primarily through one-on-one sharing	Products and services sold primarily through one-on-one sharing
Distributor consumption is a small percentage of the company's sales	Distributor consumption is a small percentage of the company's sales	Distributor consumption is a large percentage of the company's sales
Company or distributor provides a hostess program	There generally is no hostess program provided	Company generally does not provide a hostess program
Sales force comprised of 99 percent women	Sales force comprised of both men and women	Sales force comprised of both men and women with the higher percentage being men
Commissions paid on limited levels, generally three	Commissions paid to the person selling the product or on one additional level	Commissions paid on multiple levels
Retail commission is generally higher: 35-50 percent	Retail commission is generally higher: 30-50 percent	Retail commission is generally lower: 20-30 percent

Together, we achieve more and build a stronger, more powerful profession with greater understanding. Over the years, the DSWA has attracted members who believe that when another person succeeds in this business, we all win.

Why is Direct Selling Such an Amazing Opportunity?

The strength of direct selling lies in its tradition of independence, service to consumers, and commitment to entrepreneurial growth in the free enterprise system. Direct selling provides accessible business opportunities to those looking for alternative sources of income, and whose entry is not restricted by gender, age, ethnic background, education or previous experience.

Over the past ten years a shift has occurred with the substantial majority of direct sellers being women. The United States direct sales force is made up of over 87 percent women, and in other countries women represent as high as 91 percent of all direct sellers.

The products sold are as diverse as the people themselves and include:
• Cosmetics and skin care
• Laundry and personal care items
• Nutritional products
• Telecommunication and technology-oriented products
• Vacuum cleaners and home appliances
• Financial products and services
• Household decor
• Household cleaning products
• Food
• Pet care
• Toys, books, educational and scrapbooking items
• Clothing, jewelry and fashion accessories
—To mention a few product areas and more are being added regularly.

The Benefits of the Business

Direct selling provides important benefits to you who desire an opportunity to earn income and build a business of your own—and to consumers who want to enjoy intimate personalized service instead of dealing with the busy, hustle and bustle of shopping centers.

It offers an alternative to traditional employment for you who desire a flexible income earning opportunity to supplement your household income, replace the income of a full-time job and for those of you whose responsibilities or circumstances do not allow for regular part-time or full-time employment outside the home.

Women are drawn to the direct selling profession, as it provides them the ability to balance multiple priorities while meeting their financial needs. From time to time, everyone has experienced the challenges of juggling her home life with her professional life. With a direct selling business, entrepreneurs can plan *when* they want to work and *where*. Most direct sellers work from home in order to manage their schedules more effectively while taking advantage of considerable tax breaks for the home-based business entrepreneur. The tax breaks can include, but are not limited to: square footage of the home, electricity, home phone and long distance, cell phones, computer equipment, mileage and more—all expenses that are associated with your business and can equal substantial savings at tax time. For more information on the tax benefits of a home-based business, see the chapter written by Director of the DSWA Prosperity Center, Rhonda Johnson, *Run Your Business Like a Business* on page 67.

In many cases, direct selling opportunities develop into fulfilling and financially rewarding careers for those who achieve success and choose to pursue their independent direct selling business on a full-time basis.

Resources When Getting Started

There are multiple resources available to new business owners to take them through each stage of their businesses. Unlike most corporate positions, direct selling businesses are tied to each person on the team achieving his or her own success. You become more successful when you help others achieve their goals.

An added bonus is that there are people who have walked in your steps as a new business owner and are willing to take your hand and guide you down the path of success. Most companies provide training tools and starter kits filled with samples and ideas to get your business off to a solid start. Additionally, the DSWA offers a resource rich website that features teleclasses, services, information on reaching diverse markets through the DSWA Diversity Center—and much more.

The cost for an individual to start an independent direct selling business is typically very low. Usually, a modestly priced sales kit is all that is required for one to get started, and there is little or no required inventory or other cash commitments to begin. This stands in sharp contrast to franchise and other business investment opportunities, which may require substantial expenditures and expose the investor to a significant risk of loss.

Consumers Benefit As Well

Consumers benefit from direct selling because of the convenience and service provided, including personal demonstrations, product explanations, home delivery and generous satisfaction guarantees.

Moreover, direct selling provides a channel of distribution for companies with innovative or distinctive products not readily available in traditional retail stores or products that require more explanation than they would receive on a store shelf. Direct selling enhances the retail distribution infrastructure of the economy, and provides consumers with a convenient source of quality products and excellent service.

This personalized service is light years ahead of any department store personal shopper service. The direct selling customer enjoys not just shopping—but an *experience*. In today's fast-paced world, the experience plays a greater and more important role in sales each and every day.

When a customer has an *experience*, such as a scrapbooking party, memories are evoked and warm feelings become attached to the activity. The same is true for any other product whether it is skin care, candles, gourmet food or any of the other great product experiences. There is always an associated "sense" when the experience is delivered personally, be it sight, smell, touch or sound that evokes an emotional attachment, thereby creating the *experience*. The direct selling model is geared toward the building of relationships not just for loyalty, but also for a true customer experience that translates to customer satisfaction.

What sets the direct selling profession apart from other types of selling is the special relationship aspect of party plan, network marketing and person-to-person sales. Building quality relationships is the foundation of this business model that has allowed millions of people to create amazing lifestyles.

It's interesting to note that in recent years, "social networking" has taken over much of our communication, but it is the direct selling profession that has always thrived on this type of interaction for success. If anyone knows how to "social network" it is the people in this wonderful profession!

You're in the Right Place at the Right Time

Fortune magazine has called direct selling "The best kept secret in the business world. It has experienced a 94 percent growth in the last ten years... Financial experts say it's a 'recession-proof industry.'"

The power of your profession is evident. The 2008 Direct Selling Association Fact Sheet includes the following statistics:

- The U.S. was reported to have over 16 million direct sellers.
- The U.S. sales were reported to be over 30 billion dollars.
- The global sales force size was over 62 million people.
- The global direct retail sales were over 114 billion dollars.

The last few years have provided ample evidence that a direct selling, home-based business is a viable option for a strong economic future and it's not just in the United States—it's global. All over the world, record numbers of individuals are joining this amazing profession, from China to Spain to Australia and beyond, direct selling is here to stay!

The stories of lives transformed are everywhere:

- The single mom juggling two or more jobs to make ends meet, takes that same energy and pours it into her own business and finds not just financial rewards, but the courage and confidence to know she can do anything she sets her mind to.
- The new immigrant who came from a country where she sewed buttons on clothing for two cents a button while working 12 to 14 hours a day so she could afford milk and shoes for her family now owns her own home, drives a luxury car and sends money home to help her family in Mexico. In addition, many others have signed up to be on her team and are well on their way to financial independence.
- The corporate executive tired of being taken advantage of and

sacrificing her personal life for her corporate job applies her skills to her new business and has now replaced her corporate salary and takes vacations with her family.

- The school teacher who was ridiculed for following her dream of owning her own business and broke out of the teacher track to teach others to succeed!

It's all about taking the energy you put into a regular job and gifting it to yourself in the form of a business where you are your own boss!

Overcoming Obstacles to Create Success

There are certainly some things that come up that can be discouraging. However, there are many stories of real people who have overcome obstacles to achieve success in the direct selling profession. Here are seven of the most common obstacles, and stories of real people who overcame each one:

Obstacle #1: No support. Susan was excited to begin her new business. She couldn't wait to share her dreams with her family. All they had to say was… "What about us?" Her husband said "go ahead, but don't ask me to cook dinner or watch the kids while you are out partying with your friends." She explained that it wasn't partying, that she was working a party plan business to bring additional income into the family. Susan overcame this obstacle by sharing every good thing that was happening in her business, and every payday her business paid for a family adventure. Within three months it was the "family business" that she had wanted.

Obstacle #2: No training from sponsor. Connie couldn't wait to learn everything she could about how to build her new business. She was surprised when the only training by her Director was learning to talk to strangers in the mall. The Director excelled at building relationships, but had little skill in training duplicable systems. Connie quickly learned to reach out to her Director's sponsor. She read books, attended every training event she could and learned to trust her own abilities. When she took charge of her own business she advanced beyond her Director and today is in the top one percent of one of the largest companies worldwide.

Obstacle #3: No local friends or family to help jump-start the business. Darla was living in Chicago and joined a direct selling company. Within a few short weeks her husband was transferred to rural Ohio where she knew no one. She started her business with no friends or family nearby and could have quit, saying it was too difficult. Instead, she decided that although she didn't have a strong start, she was not going to give up. She built her business over time and today she is a top money earner in her company.

Obstacle #4: Money didn't stop her. Jeannie was determined to be a stay-at-home mom after the birth of her first child, shifting from being a two-income family to one that didn't cover the bills. A home-based business seemed like the perfect solution. She had a garage sale to earn her initial investment and asked her friends and family to support her in her desire to work from home. She held ten shows in her first thirty days and by the end of 100 days in business she had generated $5000 in income. She was off to a great start.

Obstacle #5: Lost job. After being downsized from his mid-level management job, John didn't know which way to turn. A friend introduced him to a network marketing company. His zealous sharing of the business caused his friends and family to question his decision and his sanity. John heard many no's and could have been discouraged and walked away. Because his network marketing company had such a positive culture and was filled with supportive individuals he stayed the course and today is a high six-figure earner.

Obstacle #6: Replacing an unsuccessful business. Sam was living the high life owning a multi-million dollar technology company. Life changed quickly as he lost everything in the aftermath of September 11. In desperation he turned to an industry he had previously rejected—network marketing. He realized in the first few weeks that he could turn this opportunity into a big business if he was willing to work the business as a full-time career. After investing 12 - 14 hours per day developing his business, he turned his life around and today enjoys the lifestyle of the rich and famous. Sam was willing to do whatever it took to create success.

Obstacle #7: Hawaiian aunties with not enough money. Two sisters were hotel maids for most of their adult lives. Everyone called them "Auntie" because they were so friendly. They were both struggling financially until someone approached them about joining a network marketing company. They got off to a slow start their first month, but knew that if they could get to their company convention they would receive the training they needed to build their businesses. They sold homemade bread along with their company products to earn their trip. When they returned home they were equipped with the knowledge and inspiration to build their businesses and shared the products and opportunity with everyone they met. Today, they are each called "Auntie" by the thousands of people on their teams.

If you are currently in a direct selling company you are to be commended. If you are looking at starting a home-based business you will find a wonderful home where you can open the doors to do business on your terms. Direct selling offers an opportunity for both men and women to use their talents and gifts to discover a future where everyone can create prosperity and an amazing lifestyle.

NICKI KEOHOHOU
Co-Founder
Direct Selling Women's Alliance

Leading the way for entrepreneurs around the globe

(808) 230-2427
info@dswa.org
www.dswa.org

Nicki began her career as a distributor in the direct selling profession more than 30 years ago after choosing to leave her teaching position. She built successful personal organizations, has spoken to direct sellers at conventions around the world, consulted to hundreds of companies and held executive positions in two companies. She co-authored the best-selling books *Build it BIG* and *More Build It BIG: 101 Insider Secrets from the Top Direct Selling Experts.*

Nicki is a graduate of the University of Illinois Chicago Network Marketing Certification program. She was recently named one of the Top 25 Business Women in her home state of Hawaii as well as one of the Top 30 Female Entrepreneurs in America. She was selected as an international "Hero for Humanity" in 2008 and named #2 in the International 2009 Women's Power 30 honoring the 30 most influential women in the direct selling profession. The award that brings her the most joy is the DSWA being recognized as the National Advocate of the Year for Working Mothers by the National Association for Moms in Business.

Nicki is the CEO and co-founder of the Direct Selling Women's Alliance and her life work is to educate and empower home-based entrepreneurs from around the globe and educate the public about this amazing profession.

Ignite Your Passion and Live with Purpose
A Guide to a Thriving Life and a Prosperous Direct Selling Business

By Shannon Bruce, CPCC, PCC, CPT

"Improve your business, your life, your relationships, your finances and your health. When you do the whole world improves."
—Mark Victor Hansen, motivational trainer, speaker, author

Think back to the day you first joined your direct sales organization. You started this business with contagious excitement and enthusiasm. You knew this opportunity would help you create the life of your dreams.

Today there may be a gap between the life you envisioned and the one you are currently living. Disappointment may be settling in and you wonder if it's really possible to create both a thriving life and a prosperous business.

In working with direct sales professionals, there are two key factors that can become roadblocks to the greater success you desire:

1. A lack of clarity. You might be doing everything you need to achieve your business vision, yet find yourself working harder than you really want to, compromising what's important in your life.

2. Comparing your success to others. You compare what you've achieved to the results of others. Instead of being motivated, you feel defeated and minimize the results you have already accomplished.

Do any of these factors ring true for you? Has your direct selling success been impacted as a result? If so, it's time to go inward to do some deeper personal work. In this chapter, you will discover the real you so you can align your business with your core, helping you to fully integrate your work into your entire life. As you and your team work through the five exercises in this guide, you will gain tools to ignite your passion, live your purpose and create direct selling prosperity.

Ignite Your Passion

Understanding the passion behind your direct sales business will reveal the inspiration that anchors you to what truly matters. Passion comes from within and is more than the enthusiasm you have for your company, business opportunity and products. It's about knowing what really makes you come alive and leveraging this in a way that creates greater meaning, adds value and makes an impact—not just for you—but also for those you influence and serve.

Solidify your personal values. You have a unique and exclusive set of personal values that define who you are at the core. Your values give rich insight into what is most important to you and what you are passionate about. This provides a solid foundation for making purposeful life choices and business decisions. Your values act as an internal compass to identify what makes you come alive as you find inner peace. When your values are excluded from your decision-making, you experience frustration and lack of fulfillment. "Community" is an example of a value. What this means to you might vary from what it means to someone else. Your values will have a sense of internal rightness with a unique definition that's exclusive to you. For instance, "community" might mean a large group of people with whom you interact on a daily basis, or it might mean a small group that you gather with less frequently but more intimately. Once you have a sense of your personal values and what they mean to you, they become an internal filter to ensure that your personal and professional decisions are aligned with your values.

Exercise #1: Discover and Define Your Motivational Core

To solidify your personal values, complete the steps below:

Step #1: Choose ten values from the list below that are most important to you. Don't over-think it. Feel free to add values that aren't on this list.

achievement	excellence	nature
acceptance	family	partnership
adventure	freedom	playfulness
beauty	fun	prosperity
catalyst	growth	quality
challenge	harmony	respect
community	influence	risk taking
connection	impact	self-expression
creativity	joy	spirituality
contribution	knowledge	wellness
discovery	leadership	wisdom
effectiveness	learning	vitality
efficiency	love	zest

Step #2: Narrow your set of values down to five from your initial list.

Step #3: Define what these top five values mean to you. Write your personal definitions. Don't censor yourself—journal whatever thoughts come to mind. For example, "harmony" might mean, "living in the flow of life; finding joy as I move with rhythm." Keep in mind there is no right or wrong answer.

15

Step #4: Consistently refer to your values list as you go through your daily activities. Assess how well you are honoring your values by ranking them on a scale of 1-10 (1 means you aren't considering your values in your decisions or activities, 10 means that you are including them). Notice which activities, choices and thoughts make you come alive and continue those. Identify what drains you and consider adjusting your attitude and behavior so your choices are in alignment with your values. Use these same core values in your business and your life to create wholeness and a sense of integration.

Reveal your truest self. As you assimilate your values into your daily life, you will notice a shift in how you approach every situation. You will be more radiant and alive. The "best you" shines through! This is your true self who exudes life and attracts others.

Exercise #2: Unveil Your True Self

To hone in on your true self complete the steps below:

Step #1: Think about the characteristics that are present when you live at your best. Write down at least three qualities that come to mind as you consider your true self.

Step #2: Visualize this woman. Imagine a movie scene in which she walks through a doorway into a room full of people. Everyone is silent as all eyes turn and notice her. Her impact is powerfully and palpably felt. What words would the people in the room use to describe her demeanor, her impact and the energy she brings? Write down at least three additional characteristics that describe this woman's essence.

Step #3: Read this list of descriptors aloud. Immerse yourself by repeatedly verbalizing the list. Feel into her heart. Experience her presence internally as you visualize her being right there in the room with you.

Step #4: As you connect with her, imagine this woman has a name that describes who she is at the core. Allow your heart to guide you as you creatively capture all of these qualities into an adjective or phrase that describes her. Don't over-think her name.

Examples of the "true names" of women with whom I've worked are: Passionate Radiance, Alive and On Purpose, and Brilliantly Sassy.

Step #5: Imagine wearing a nametag each day with the name of your true self on it. Be this woman. Let her make the choices for your life and business, using your personal values as a guide. Notice the impact you have and continue to make changes needed to fully ignite your passion.

Live Your Purpose

As you honor your values and you live from your truest self, your passion is ignited and you find a greater purpose for your direct sales business. This purpose goes beyond booking, selling and recruiting to connecting with the greater gift that lives within you. This is your unique purpose for being here. As this gift is opened in service to others, there's a subtle transition from "how can this business help me" to "what contribution can I make using my business as the vehicle." This subtle yet powerful shift is profound because it allows you to connect with this greater purpose while leaving a legacy that impacts your family, your community and the world.

Articulate your deepest motivation. It's important to know why you are here on this earth, living this life, because it will help you discover the purpose for your direct sales business. Notice the change in focus to "why you are here" from "why you are in your direct sales business." Shifting the focus in this way takes the spotlight off how you will benefit from your direct sales business and places attention on what you bring to others through it. This is an important concept to understand. Let me clarify my point by sharing a real-life example:

One of my clients now understands that her purpose is to "celebrate women, children and families." Reflecting on her life, she noticed many people affected by the disease of cancer so she decided to use her direct sales business as a fundraising vehicle for the American Cancer Society. She talks about this at her parties and shares her passion to impact the lives of women, children and families. Because of this shift, she now finds greater purpose in her work and her direct sales business is flourishing. She is touching lives and contributing by giving a percentage of her profits to fund cancer research.

Exercise #3: Reveal Your Purpose

To discover your purpose, explore the following steps:

Step #1: Answer the following questions:
1. What impact do you wish to have on your family, your community and others as you serve them through your business?
2. How will being a part of this business change you and your life?
3. How will others be changed?

Step #2: Journal your thoughts and note recurring themes. Some examples of purpose are "helping women find health and wellness from the inside and out," "empowering others to achieve abundance through personal and professional success" and "leading women to emotional, physical and financial freedom." Consider using this as a personal tag line for your business. For my work as a coach, I use "connecting you to your greater purpose."

Step #3: Use this theme to evaluate your personal and professional choices. This will ensure what you do is in alignment with your deepest "why."

Determine your personal life mission and impact. Now that you understand your purpose, you can name your personal mission. When you fulfill your life mission, it results in a positive and meaningful impact on the lives of others. It is unique to you and encompasses your whole life—not just your business. Consequently, it helps guide you through all areas, bringing integration and harmony to both your life and work. Your mission reminds you of your strengths and passions, enabling you to make the best decisions.

Your mission statement is a concise, powerful phrase beginning with the word "to," which reveals your personal impact. It's designed to be used with your values and true self to measure the quality of the results you achieve. As you live out your mission, you will see your influence in the lives of others, which happens naturally because it's coming from the core of who you are. Living your mission and creating a favorable effect on others is like living in your "sweet spot" where you achieve greater results with less effort.

Exercise #4: Proclaim Your Mission

Take some time now to define your personal life mission statement.

Step #1: Consider the following questions as you explore your mission statement:
• When your true self is present, what impact do you have on others?
• How are others transformed by your true self?
• What themes are emerging?

Step #2: Write out your mission statement starting with the word "to." Examples of mission statements are "to bring joy and life to others," "to create and nurture life-changing community wherever I go" and "to inspire others to authenticity and purpose." Whatever you come up with, make sure it's all-encompassing to include the many activities that happen throughout your life roles of wife, mom, business owner, woman, sister, friend and daughter.

Step #3: Post your mission statement on your wall and read it daily. Use it as a personal affirmation.

Step #4: Share your mission statement with your spouse and your team. Ask people to hold you accountable to living your mission with intention and purpose.

Step #5: Evaluate the impact you are having in your life using your mission statement. Make ongoing choices that support your mission so that the quality of your life and your business results continue to improve.

Create Direct Selling Prosperity

My goal for you is that you create a thriving life and a prosperous business. I've seen it many times as women connect with their passion and purpose, because this place of authentic aliveness creates prosperity! Author Frederick Buechner reinforced this point when he said, *"Find where your great joy and the world's great need intersect, and that, most likely is where you belong."*

The true measure of your success comes from within as your perception of prosperity is expanded to include both your passion and purpose.

Integrate your passion and purpose to define personal success. To create *your personal definition of success*, include your passion and purpose to help hone in on the designation that fits for you. You might be tempted to focus on outward measurements of success, such as income level, team size and the number of contests you've won. These are the results of being successful rather than the definition of success.

As you integrate what you learn about yourself from this chapter, your personal definition of success will emerge. Identifying what truly matters to you will help you define *your* success in the world. As you apply your personal definition to your life and business, it will lead to greater internal fulfillment and create improved external results.

Exercise #5: Name Your Success

Follow the steps below to define personal success for you:

Step #1: Consider what makes you feel successful. Exclude outward measurements as you write down ways that you evaluate your successes. You might measure your success by how much you are enjoying your creativity, or how nice a person you are being at any given moment, or the ways your business has allowed you to transform the lives of others.

Step #2: Use your personal definition to assess your current level of impact in life and business. What adjustments do you need to make? Make the necessary changes that will help you ignite your passion as you live with purpose. In doing so, your success will improve based on your personal criteria.

Step #3: Notice the external effect on your life as you evaluate your success using internal measurements. How much is your team expanding? How is the quality of your relationships changing? How much has your income increased? Continue to make changes that ignite your passion so you live your mission while increasing your direct selling prosperity.

Expand your perspective of prosperity. According to Webster's Dictionary, prosperity is "a successful, flourishing, or thriving condition." Typically, we think of prosperity in the context of our finances, which is certainly one aspect of being prosperous.

Expand your definition to include not only financial prosperity, but

21

also emotional, physical and spiritual prosperity. If you're willing to enlarge your definition, you can stay connected to your passion and purpose and leverage everything you've learned thus far to create a prosperous business and a thriving life.

Be Big, Be Bold and Be YOU!

In one of the coach training classes I attended, participants were instructed to visualize what their life billboards would say when living authentically. My billboard said: "Be Big, Be Bold and Be YOU!" This personal affirmation continues to call me forth to greatness. It also reminds me to integrate all that I've learned about myself in the creation of my genuine and inspired life.

Now that you've learned more about yourself through the exercises included in this chapter, what would the billboard of your life say about you?

As you contemplate this, keep in mind that when you discover who you are on the inside you will find your unique personal definition of success, aligned with the heart of who you are. Your values and your true self can be fully expressed, igniting your passion which guides you to your greater purpose. With your deeper reasons and mission clear, you can leverage your unique gift to create direct selling prosperity and leave a lasting legacy to others. From this authentic place, anything is possible!

As you go through this process, remember that life is a journey, not a destination. Don't feel pressured to find exact answers to the questions included here because there are no right or wrong responses. Pay attention to what's being revealed as you go forth to transform your life and your business. It's time to ignite your passion, live your purpose and create direct selling prosperity!

SHANNON BRUCE, CPCC, PCC, CPT

Connecting you to your greater purpose!

(360) 308-8292
shannon@yourgreaterpurpose.com
www.yourgreaterpurpose.com
www.shannonbruce.com

Shannon is a catalyst for life change and a Mompreneur Success Coach committed to helping self-employed women break through barriers, reconnect with what matters and achieve exceptional lives and extraordinary businesses. Her professional coach training through The Coaches Training Institute helps women rediscover what's on the inside to gain clarity and purpose, while building strong foundations that support thriving personal lives *and* prosperous careers.

As a former CPA, Corporate Regional Operations Manager and direct sales leader, Shannon understands the systems needed to create a sustainable business. As a single mom, she also knows the importance of building a solid platform based on what truly matters.

Blending a heart-centered coaching approach with practical tools, Shannon helps women integrate their values, identity and mission to build meaningful lives and purposeful careers. Whether speaking or coaching, her facilitation consistently provides a safe, nurturing and challenging space for others to explore and stretch into more of their truest selves.

Shannon currently leads, coaches, trains and inspires women in both individual and group venues. Through her wisdom and encouragement, women experience lasting transformation that allows them to boldly go after their inspired life with courage, confidence and authenticity.

23

Developing an Abundant and Profitable Mindset

By Marcy Stahl

What will have the biggest impact on your business over the next year? Think about that for a minute. Did you answer "the economy"? Or maybe "social media"? The true answer is, "the voices inside your head." This may seem strange, but it's true.

Here are some of the things that those voices can say:
- *"You can't do that."*
- *"No one can make money that way."*
- *"People don't want to listen to me; they don't care about my offer."*
- *"Wealthy people are uncaring and greedy."*
- *"If I become successful, I'll become a different person and thus lose my friends and family."*

It's exhausting and depressing just reading that list! These are all examples of limiting beliefs that give you a negative mindset and interfere with your ability to build a successful business.

Develop a Top Mindset
The top women in direct sales have the top mindsets. When you have been around the most successful women in your direct sales company, you've undoubtedly noticed how relaxed and self-confident they are and how they are present in the moment, even while they're leading very busy lives.

A profitable and abundant mindset is the biggest contributor to their success. They are very conscious of the power of their mindset, and continually work at developing and maintaining it. They read books or listen to audio recordings on topics like the law of attraction, how the brain works or on building a business. Some have a spiritual practice that they incorporate into each day.

They didn't get super-extra-special training from their direct sales company, nor do they have 30 hours in each day instead of 24. They all started out at the same place as you, with many of the same limiting beliefs in their head.

They may have started out thinking: *"I don't think I can make a lot of money"* or *"I can't get this business going"* or *"People won't pay attention to me."* Along their mindset journey, they shifted to a mindset of: *"There's plenty of abundance in the universe. There's always someone who wants to hear about what I offer. Money comes to me easily."* If these women, who started out just like you, can do the work of shifting their mindset, then so can you.

A Successful Mindset Starts with You

The biggest change you can make in your business is to change yourself. The benefits are huge:

- Your business becomes more successful, which translates into more income and opportunities.
- You feel more at ease in your life.
- You become the kind of person who attracts other people. People want to be around you because they feel something special in your presence.
- It helps you accomplish your purpose in your work. That is the biggest reason to have an abundant and profitable mindset.

Five Steps to Creating and Maintaining an Abundant and Profitable Mindset

"Thinking small isn't hard. It's just a habit.
A habit with consequences. Same for thinking big."
—Mike Dooley, American entrepreneur

1. Make a conscious choice to change how you want to think, and most importantly, feel in your business. To implement a change in your habits, you have to have some energy behind that choice. Are you totally committed, in that "can't-wait-to-start-and-know-just-what-you-want" way? Are you thinking, "These ideas could be true but I'm not certain. It sounds possible, and a little intriguing." You can start to change your thinking from a place of curiosity and exploration or from a place of total commitment. Either way will work. Right now make a commitment to yourself to develop your abundant and profitable mindset in order to fulfill your purpose and succeed in your business.

2. Decide where you want to be. Maybe you already know where you want to be, or whom you want to emulate. Do you want to be on stage at your company's next conference? Do you want to make enough money to send your children to a private school? Do you want to become the kind of successful and inspiring team leader you see in your upline?

Whatever you decide, write it down and cut out a picture for your visualization board. Get really clear on what you want your life to look like and write a vivid description—now. This is really important. Do not read any further until you have gotten clear on what you want your life to look like.

If you're not sure about your goals, try this question: What are the qualities you'd like to experience in your life? Ease? Abundance? Beauty? Fun? You can often gain clarity on your goals and life vision by first exploring your values. For more on choosing your top values visit Shannon Bruce's chapter, *Ignite Your Passion and Live with Purpose,* on page 13.

Next, get your subconscious enrolled in your success:

- Get all your senses involved. What are the sights, sounds, and smells associated with your vision of success?
- Make it emotional. Numbers alone are not motivating. Having a new house with more space for the kids is motivating. Being able to quit your job because you have replaced your income is motivating. Seeing yourself running a meeting in your living room with thirty enthusiastic direct sellers filling the space is motivating. *Feel* your vision.
- Visualize each step along the way. If you know the steps leading to your vision, visualize yourself performing them. That's what Olympic athletes do. If you're not sure how to achieve your vision, then visualize the results and you'll gradually fill in the process along the way. If you do not want to wait until then, start talking to others who have achieved what you are working on and ask them what steps they took.
- Review your pictures, vision board and/or your written goals often—ideally twice a day. Just like the way to get to Carnegie Hall is through practice, focusing on your vision is practice for achieving your vision. It also sets your mental antenna to pick up opportunities and next steps that will help you accomplish your goals.

3. Get clear on your money attitude. Most likely, your money attitude is either what you inherited from your family of origin or it's the total opposite of your family's attitude.

- **Is money hard to come by?** I come from a family of midwestern farmers. Collectively, my family members envision earning a living, not building wealth.
- **Is money hard to hold on to?** Do you think: *"I'm not good with money"*?
- **Is it hard for you to spend money?** My grandmother was a child of the Depression and she could not bring herself to buy three pairs of shoes at one time, regardless of whether she needed them or not.

What does wealth mean to you? Do you believe rich people are mean, greedy and snooty? If you believe that making money is hard or complicated or it will turn you into a bad person, you are going to have a very hard time letting yourself become successful.

4. Get clear on how you define success. Culturally, success is often defined as hard work and struggle. If you're not struggling, can you be successful? How do you define work and success? What was the meaning of work and success in your family?

If your parents divorced because your father or mother was always working, you could consciously or unconsciously believe that success can cause marriages to fail.

My past work experience led to this belief: success means working long hours, which ultimately means my health suffers. I couldn't be successful when I believed it was going to ruin my health and my quality of life.

- Can success come to you easily or does it have to be a struggle in order to be labeled success?
- Can you be successful working part-time or does success require full-time or even overtime effort?
- Does work mean a steady income with benefits or does work need to be meaningful and fit with your life purpose?

Your definition of success is right for you—just make sure you know what it is. If it's the opposite of your family or cultural definition of success, then take a minute to check in with yourself emotionally to see whether that difference is creating any internal conflict, which can lead to unconscious limiting beliefs, stopping you in your tracks.

5. Uncover how you might sabotage yourself. We've all shot ourselves in the foot at some point in our lives. We each have a different style for doing this and a different timing for when we do it. Do you feel you can't ask for what you truly want, so you don't even get started? Do you feel you're not qualified or don't deserve it, so you fail along the way, even though the goal is in sight? Or do you achieve your goal, and then throw it away?

If you truly don't know your style of self-sabotage, ask a trusted friend or family member who has your best interests at heart.

Another great resource is *Stop Self-Sabotage* by Pat Pearson, published by McGraw Hill in 2009. She describes where self-sabotage comes from, lists some common patterns and provides concrete ideas on how to get out from under those patterns.

Four Steps to Solidifying an Abundant and Profitable Mindset

"Do not be impatient with your seemingly slow progress. Do not try to run faster than you presently can. If you are studying, reflecting and trying, you are making progress whether you are aware of it or not. A traveler walking the road in the darkness of night is still going forward. Someday, some way, everything will break open, like the natural unfolding of a rosebud."
—Vernon Howard, American author

Here's where you're developing new habits to replace the old. Initially, it feels awkward, and requires conscious attention—like driving for the first time. Just like driving, after you get good at it, it becomes automatic. Here are four steps to help you replace old habits with new ones as you develop an abundant mindset and get where you want to go:

1. Practice great self-care. This includes getting enough sleep, eating well, exercising, connecting with nature, going for your health check-ups, taking care of yourself when you're not feeling well—and more. If you find it difficult or impossible to take care of yourself, that's a clue that you have negative beliefs about what you deserve to have in life and how you deserve to be treated. What can you do to improve your self-care?

2. Go on an information diet. When you want to improve your health and fitness, you watch what goes in your mouth. So, when you want to improve your mental health and fitness, watch what goes in your brain.

Skip the news—it's almost all negative. Instead of watching the news and feeling anxiety about hurricanes, terrorism and the economy, get involved in your key areas of concern or decide to focus your energy elsewhere and move on.

In place of the news, spend time listening to great speakers and reading self-development books. This is one of the practices of top women in direct sales. Their reading and listening is highly directed. They make a conscious choice every day about the ideas and information to which they expose themselves.

3. Be aware of your self-talk. Thoughts become things. What you focus on expands. The total chain of your thoughts, one after the other throughout the day, determines how you feel. This can be very subtle. One negative thing you see or think starts you remembering some other negative thing and then it's all downhill.

In contrast, one positive thing can remind you of something else, you feel great; you make your calls and feel good that you are helping people. It's all reinforced, and you wind up the day feeling fantastic! Pay close attention to your daily self-talk. Eliminate all negative self-talk.

4. Be around like-minded, positive people. If your goal was to quit gambling, smoking or doing drugs, you'd stop hanging out in places where those activities went on. You'd stop spending time with people who did those things.

If you want to quit negativity, stop hanging out with people who are not on the path you're on, or don't believe in your ability to achieve what you want. You deserve positive relationships in your life. Let go of relationships that bring you down and do not support your success.

Three Tips for Maintaining Positive Change

"You will never change your life until you change something you do daily. The secret of success is found in your daily action."
—John Maxwell, American pastor, leadership expert and author

You'll need help maintaining this new way of thinking over the long term. Your old thoughts and habits have been reinforced in your brain many, many times. In the same way you can eventually drive or cook automatically without paying attention, eventually you can also think and respond to situations in a positive way automatically.

If you find yourself slipping back into negative ways of thinking, which can happen to all of us from time to time, you'll probably find that you've stopped doing some of the practices listed above. You may have started letting the news back into your life, or started spending time with negative people again, or slacked off on your self-care. When you notice this happening, recommit and revisit what we have already discussed.

1. Shift your energy when you are down. The journey to an abundant mindset is really a journey toward greater wholeness. There's no final destination involved; the journey itself is the work and the reward. As you create your abundant and profitable mindset, you will consistently be confronting your old patterns of self-sabotage coming up in new guises. You'll need to have tools that are guaranteed to turn your thinking around.

When you feel down or see old patterns arise:
- Remind yourself of the results your old patterns gave you. Those results were probably not greater love, ease and abundance.
- Look for the lesson in the situation. What can you learn from it? How are you different now? Is there a new way you can look at the situation?
- Take credit for your accomplishments. Remind yourself how far you've come.
- If being self-critical has been a problem, forgive yourself.
- Most importantly, get back on the path to abundance and to your vision of success.

2. Maintain a daily spiritual practice. Cultivate a spiritual practice that connects you with whatever higher source in which you believe. Whether you pray or meditate or spend time in nature—whatever your practice is—make sure you spend time every day connecting with that energy. It will continuously sustain you. Connecting with spirit will give you energy for what's next and clarity on your next steps and will help you stay connected with your purpose.

3. Celebrate! You are one awesome, forward-thinking woman! Every change you make—even before it bears fruit—is a reason to celebrate. After you write down your goals or the qualities you want in your life—celebrate. Have you done some work on your money beliefs? Celebrate!

One of the reasons many people are so attracted to young children is how effortlessly they find joy and fun in anything. Make sure you have joy and fun in your life. Part of that is celebrating!

It Is All Yours for the Asking

You can have whatever mindset you want, so why not choose a profitable and abundant one? As your mindset becomes more abundant, you'll find that you feel more at ease—more relaxed and less stressed. You'll connect with others so much more easily, because your focus will shift from *"how does this help me?"* to *"how can I help this person?"*

The dynamics of your relationships with customers and prospects will shift. Everything will start to feel effortless, things will just happen or you will see that they were meant to be. You'll feel like the universe is getting aligned with your desires—as in fact it is. Everything becomes easier, and wonderful people and opportunities turn up out of nowhere. It all starts the minute you begin to shift your mindset. Why not start today?

MARCY STAHL

Helping women entrepreneurs achieve world domination—one business at a time!

(703) 820-9520
marcy@marcystahl.com
www.marcystahl.com

Marcy Stahl's passion is helping women entrepreneurs achieve the successful lifestyle they want. She knows that the top entrepreneurs have the top mindsets. Her mission is to help every entrepreneur develop a profitable and abundant mindset.

She helps her clients move from frustration and struggle to a steady flow of clients and team members, while feeling a sense of confidence and abundance.

She uses an eight-step process that addresses the outer world of business: marketing strategies, recruiting and leadership, as well as the inner game of entrepreneurship: managing your energy and cultivating a powerful mindset.

She loves to work with women in direct sales who are building teams. She helps leaders build better teams by:
• Developing a more abundant and successful mindset
• Recruiting more effectively and recruiting more business-builders
• Motivating and communicating effectively with their team

Marcy is a serial entrepreneur. Previously, she co-founded and managed a government contracting firm that earned over $1M in annual revenues. She holds a BS with honors and an MS in Computer Science from George Mason University. Prior to coaching, she spent 21 years in the corporate world in technology.

The Responsibility Game
Your Key to Amazing Direct Selling Success

By Celine Egan

In this chapter you are going to focus on responsibility—and why, if you do not take responsibility for yourself and your actions, nothing will change for you and you will not get what it is you are after. This is important for your life, and important for getting the most out of your direct selling business.

Recognize that No One Else Can Do It for You

Most of us have been conditioned to blame something outside of ourselves for the parts of our lives we don't like. We blame our parents, our bosses, our friends, the media, the culture we live in, our co-workers, our clients, our spouse, the weather, the economy, our astrological chart, our upline, our downline and our lack of money—anyone or anything that we can pin the blame on. We never want to look at where the real responsibility lies—with ourselves.

It is time to stop looking outside yourself for the answers to why you haven't created the life and results you want, for it is you who creates the life and results you want, and it is you who creates the quality of the life you lead and the results you produce. You are responsible—no one else!

Taking 100 percent responsibility means that you acknowledge that you create everything that happens to you. It means you understand that you are the cause of all of your experiences. If you want to be really successful, and I know you do, then you will have to give up blaming and complaining and take total responsibility for your life—that means all your results, both your successes and your failures. That is the prerequisite for creating a life of success. It is only by acknowledging that you have created everything up until now that you can take charge of creating the future you want. If you realize that you have created your current conditions, then you can un-create them and re-create them at will.

Are you willing to take 100 percent responsibility for your life? I am and I did. Once I decided that I wanted to move up in my business I took responsibility for the results. I made the calls each day, I did the follow-up, I offered everyone the opportunity to do business with me by either joining my team, hosting a demo or buying my product. By finally taking responsibility for my own success I was able to move up to managership within a couple of months and qualify for my company car six weeks later. I did this all while working a full-time job as an office manager with two children under two. Taking responsibility for your life is so empowering.

"If you keep on doing what you have always done, you will keep on getting what you have always got."
—W.L. Bateman

Play the "Responsibility Game" Above the Line

You are playing above the line when you are taking 100 percent responsibility. Playing above the line is taking responsibility for all of your actions, your successes and your failures. When you are playing below the line you fall into blame, shame and justification. What does this mean?

Blame. This is when you notice yourself blaming others for what is going on in your life. You are late for an appointment and you blame the traffic. Did you take responsibility and leave on time or allow extra time for the traffic? Or you blame your team for not reaching a sales target. Did you communicate the goal to them, did you track the goal and did you give continuous feedback? Maybe you blame your spouse for an unhappy marriage. How do you model the behavior that you would like to see in your marriage? Give up blaming. It's a waste of time. No matter how much fault you find with another and regardless of how much you blame him or her, it will not change you.

Shame. This is when you listen to that negative voice in your head that tells you that you are stupid, you can't achieve that or you always do things that way. That voice is only trying to protect you and keep you in your comfort zone. Acknowledge it, and then take responsibility to step into the unknown anyway and learn new things. It is better to fail at something than to never have tried.

Justify. This is when you decide to tell a story around why you have or have not done something. The reality is that stories waste time and most people are not interested. They only want to know if you are going to do it and when. For example, you have not done your five business building calls for the day and you committed to your coach or manager that you were going to do them, or you didn't drop an order off to a client. They only want to know what you did and if not, when are you going to do it. They don't really want to know that the washing needed doing or the kids where sick. This may seem harsh, but it is amazing how much more focused you become when you "play above the line." Things get done and you will find that you have so much more free time.

You only have control over three things in your life—the thoughts you think, the images you visualize, and the actions you take (your behavior). How you use these three things determines everything you experience.

You Are in Charge

The bottom line is that you are the one who is creating your life the way it is. The life you currently live is a result of your past thoughts and actions. You are in charge of your current thoughts and your present feelings. You are in charge of what you say and what you do. You are also in charge of what goes into your mind—the books and magazines you read, the movies and television shows you watch and the people with whom you hang out. Every action is under your control. To be more successful, all you have to do is act in ways that produce more of what you want.

How does this work when it comes to your direct sales business?

Blame. Do you take responsibility for the success of your business or do you drop below the line into blame—blaming your team members for not performing?

Shame. Do you shame yourself for not doing your calls?

Justify. Do you justify why you have no time to follow up on your leads?

Ask yourself: how can I take responsibility for my business, how can I play above the line? Do I look each day at how I can make a difference with my prospects, my customers and my team members? Taking responsible action in each area of your business will reap the rewards you want.

Be Responsible for Building Great Business Relationships

Do you attend networking events to expand your network and in turn your business? Do you follow up after each event? Remember that it is about you taking responsibility for building the relationships with those prospects, not the other way around.

There is a certain amount of work that goes into building relationships. As Dr. Misner, founder of Business Network International, the largest referral networking organization in the world, says, "It is net *work*!" After attending a networking function, I put any cards or notes from that event into one designated basket. They do not move out of there until I have followed up. That can be either an email, a handwritten card or phone call. I touch base to let them know that it was lovely to meet them, and that if there is anything I can do to help them in their business, to just let me know. Again, I am taking responsibility for building the relationship by offering to help them, focusing more on what I can do for them rather than what they can do for me. I am building a relationship, and I am being responsible for following up with them, not sitting there waiting for them to call me.

Be Responsible for Your Own Training

Training is key to the growth of your direct selling business: training on business skills like booking, selling and recruiting, as well as personal development training. Yes, you want to learn business skills. You also want to grow personally. The more you invest in improving yourself the more it will reflect in how effective you are in your business. Consider personal development training on communication skills, relationship skills, self-esteem or wherever else you feel you can use a boost.

Do you take responsibility for attending professional development training, joining in on company teleclasses, reviewing online educational courses provided by your company or those put on by other organizations? Reading this book is an excellent step. Books are an invaluable source of personal and professional development.

Take responsibility for the growth of any aspect of yourself that you want to enhance or upgrade. Ask yourself where you can use a little business or personal development training.

Be Responsible for Asking for What You Want

This is a great skill to learn. When you ask for what you want you might just be surprised and get it. It has been my experience that when I make a habit of asking for what I want, the results come. Ask for demos, ask for the sale, ask people to join your business and ask for the referral. Will the answer always be yes? Probably not, but there is more chance of a yes when you actually ask.

Be Responsible for the Language You Use

This is so important! The language we use, both internally in our head and externally to those around us, can determine the quality of our lives. Be the type of person that uses empowering positive language. Use language that takes responsibility for your actions rather than blaming or shaming others and making them wrong. Use the words *"I choose"* or *"I want"* rather than *"I have to"* or *"I need to."* When you say, "I choose to..." it is empowering because you are in control, rather than feeling disempowered about what you have to do. Every day success comes down to a series of choices. Each morning you choose to get out of bed, you can choose to have a great day and you choose the attitude you will bring to your business. Choosing how you speak—to yourself and to others—can make a huge difference in your mindset and how you are perceived in the world.

Be Responsible for Your Word

Another area of responsibility that is very important is keeping your agreements. When you step up to leadership in your direct selling business you are in fact making an agreement with your downline. This agreement includes providing training for them, being accessible (within reason) and continuing to provide the service you would expect to give and receive. There are written and unwritten, as well as spoken and unspoken, agreements in all areas of our lives. Be the person who always takes responsibility for honoring those agreements. By doing this you show yourself to be an ethical person who others will want to be around.

Sometimes you will need to re-make an agreement. You may find that you are not going to be able to accomplish something by the time you promised. Rather than being out of communication, consider checking in with the person to whom you gave your word, and getting their agreement to a new deadline. This is much better than not confronting the situation, feeling guilty, and blaming yourself for failing to keep your word.

Be Responsible for Learning to Use the Word "No"

Sometimes you need to be kind to yourself and learn to say no. When you are a person who is known to get things done, you may often be called on to do lots of things—some that will serve you and others and some that will not. Learn to say no in the moment, while giving yourself permission to change your mind if you so choose later. Learning to do this means that you stop saying yes as a reaction and getting bogged down with too many responsibilities. This way you are taking responsibility for going away and giving the request consideration in your own time and coming back to say you are available if you feel the desire to do so. You will find that you have so much more control over your life this way.

Be Responsible for Your Schedule

Schedule everything into your diary or planner. Put down the tasks that only you can do because they call for your expertise or are dependent on a relationship you have built. Delegate—or even don't do—everything else.

What you want to remember is that you cannot manage time—you can only manage yourself. Everyone has the same amount of time— 24 hours in the day. However, some people get a lot more done than others. Here's what I do to maximize my effectiveness during the day.

I evaluate every item on my to-do list by:
• Do/schedule
• Delegate
• Dump

If some task presents itself—and I mean even the ironing, the shopping or the cooking—I ask myself three questions:
• Can I, or do I want to do this now? If the answer is yes and my planner is clear, then I do it. If my planner is not clear I schedule it in for a later time. Once I have scheduled it, I don't give it another thought until the relevant time.
• Is it something that doesn't take my expertise? If so, then can I delegate it, and to whom? I then delegate it right away, or schedule in the time when I will communicate to someone else about it.
• Is it unimportant and really doesn't need my—or anyone else's— expertise or attention? Then I dump it.

Do check out the two other chapters in this book that will support you in mastering your schedule: Martha Staley's chapter, *Managing Life as a Direct Selling Superstar*, on page 47 and Anne Nelson's chapter, *An Organized Office*, on page 57. I encourage you to read and implement their many brilliant ideas.

Set time aside to look at what you are currently doing. Note what habits you have implemented in your business that may not be supporting you and take responsibility for making changes in your life. Notice when you drop below the line into blame, shame and justification and get yourself back above the line into taking responsibility and moving in action towards your goals. Pay attention to your self-talk and your communications with others. Most of all, take responsibility for your happiness and living a fulfilling life.

CELINE EGAN
The Complete You Coaching Company

+61 409166070
Celine@tcy.com.au
www.tcy.com.au
www.acceleratewomen.com

Celine Egan is a master of self-management. As the owner of two successful businesses, a board member of a registered training operator, the Director of Operations for DSWA Australia/NZ, as well as a wife and mother of three, she knows what it takes to manage a complex life and to live "above the line."

Celine, wanting the flexibility to work around a young family, took the leap into the direct sales and network marketing industry with great vigor, and has never looked back. Today, with over 25 years experience behind her, Celine now provides individuals and organizations with training, coaching and mentoring programs in direct sales, time-management, self-management and goal-setting.

Celine is a firm believer in ongoing education and has studied under some of the most innovative training and business minds in the world today.

She is passionate about making sure that the people with whom she works walk away knowing that their time has been put to good use and they are armed with the skills, resources and tools to succeed in their chosen professions.

Managing Life as a Direct Selling Superstar

By Martha Staley, CDC

"I read and walked for miles at night along the beach, writing bad blank verse and searching for someone wonderful who would step out of the darkness and change my life. It never crossed my mind that that person could be me."
—Anna Quindlen, Pulitzer Prize-winning author

As a leader and coach in the direct selling profession, when I ask consultants in what areas of their business and life they feel they need the most help, the resounding answer is time management. I certainly appreciate this answer, as I experienced the exact same feelings when I began my direct selling career over two decades ago.

Like most new consultants, I was excited to get started and loved everything about my direct sales business. Quickly I was thrilled to realize that through parties and sharing the business opportunity, I was not only earning an income and having fun but I was making a difference for the hosts, guests and my team members—all at the same time. As wonderful as that sounds, the truth is there were many days when I was overwhelmed, out of touch, burned out and simply worn out because I didn't have an efficient time management system that empowered me to include all of the important aspects of my life and gave me time to refuel myself so that I could be the best for those that I loved the most.

If you are experiencing or have ever experienced those same feelings as a direct selling superstar, I want to assure you that managing your business and your life doesn't have to be overwhelming or challenging. From my direct selling business and life experience, I discovered that effective time management is about making the right choices with the time you are given. When you understand that you are responsible for your choices and begin to make your daily decisions based on your values and priorities, it will lead to experiencing the maximum personal, family and business benefits and the success that you desire in your business and your life.

This chapter will give you information that empowers you and gives you permission to make the right choices: the choices that are the best for you, your family and your business based on your own unique life circumstances, values and priorities, rather than using a one-size-fits-all cookie cutter time management system.

What choices can you make that will make it possible to have enough time in your day to accomplish and achieve your business goals? What choices can you make that will give you the time to enjoy your family and the benefits of your direct selling business? How do you determine what strategies are the best for you to incorporate into your daily life and that will enable you to create the business of your dreams? No matter where you are in your direct selling profession, a beginner or a seasoned leader, the following information will help you discover strategies that are a perfect fit for you and that you can easily adapt as your life and direct selling business evolve.

You and Your Life Puzzle Pieces

Your life is unique to you. Even though you have the same number of hours in your day as the next person, how you decide to spend that time is based on your values and the level of priority that you assign to the different aspects of your life. Identifying and defining your personal life puzzle pieces makes it possible for you to assess their importance, give them priority and determine the amount of time that you will allow for them in your daily schedule. When you are aware of the importance that you place on each individual piece, and what role it plays in your daily life, you can formulate various strategies that can be incorporated into your personal time management system.

Consider that you have five main life puzzle pieces: You, Spiritual, Relationships, Health and Career. When you look at the career piece, if you are one of those direct sellers that also has a full-time job, make sure you allow for that in your planning. I encourage you to take some serious time to evaluate each of these pieces and clarify the values and priorities that you assign to each of them. This exercise will assist you in defining where and how often you place them in your daily, weekly or monthly calendar and how much time you choose to spend on each.

1. You. Ask yourself, who are you really? And what do you need? Do you have a clear vision of what you want your business and life to be like one year from now and a strategy to achieve it? Are you proactive in planning your daily and weekly priorities? Do you take time every day for yourself and model balance and self care for your family, friends and team members? These are important questions to ask as you journey to find the ideal way to manage your life as a direct selling superstar. Your answers to these questions influence the choices you make in your everyday life. These choices will either move you forward toward your goals or keep you from achieving them.

2. Spiritual. *"Your vision will become clear only when you look into your heart. Who looks outside, dreams. Who looks inside, awakens."* —Carl Jung, Swiss psychiatrist. Because we are a combination of mind, body and soul, it is necessary to nourish our spiritual well-being as well as our mental and physical wellness. Here are a few suggested ways to become a more spiritual being:

• Daily devotions

• Meditation

• Journaling

Taking time to listen to what your heart has to say will clear your mind and improve your connection with yourself. As a result, you will find that you are more focused and make better business and personal decisions. What will you do to make sure your spiritual life gets daily attention?

3. Relationships. The five key elements to having and maintaining healthy relationships are trust, acknowledgement, respect, being accountable for your commitments, and how you communicate with others. Many of life's most precious memories and experiences are provided by the relationships that you build with others. Keeping in mind that your relationships with others are directly related to the relationship that you have with yourself; do you respect and trust yourself by keeping commitments with yourself? On a scale of 1–10, ask yourself: How do I rate in my relationships with myself, individual family members, friends and team members?

• What is working in your relationships and what needs to be fixed?

• If you are not satisfied with the level of your relationships, what are some things that you can do to improve them?

4. Health. By taking special care of your physical and mental health you will be empowered and better prepared for life's everyday challenges. Your physical and emotional health is affected by your daily activities and the choices that you make. For optimal physical health, consider the benefits of regular exercise, plenty of rest and good nutrition. You can boost your mental health by cultivating a good support system from family and friends, setting goals and challenging yourself to be the best that you can be on a daily basis. What are those things you want to include in your schedule every day to ensure optimal health?

5. Career. As you develop into a direct selling superstar, you will experience different stages of your career. A few strategies to consider that will improve managing your life during these stages and assist you in maintaining the career-life balance that you desire are:

• Setting boundaries between your career and personal life
• Setting office hours
• Rethinking the way you do things
• Learning to delegate and giving yourself permission to say no to opportunities that will not move you forward toward your career and personal goals.

Direct Selling Superstar Strategies

I often say, "Life happens on a daily basis." And yes, sometimes the things that happen are out of your control. However, when you decide to be in control of your daily choices and you are the center of your life puzzle pieces, you will experience more joy, abundance and goals achieved in both your business and your personal life.

There are three key strategies that I recommend to enhance the way you manage your life as a direct selling superstar:

1. Make yourself a priority in your own life. Contrary to popular belief, making yourself a priority in your own life is not a selfish thing to do. It is not only a valuable gift to give yourself but it will have lasting benefits for those that you love the most. Refueling your soul and your spirit on a daily basis is vital to balancing the success of your career, personal and family life. Even giving yourself fifteen minutes of priority time will make a huge difference in the way you relate to others and how you perform during the day. You can optimize your daily planning by asking yourself the following questions:

- What absolutely needs to be included in my day for me to consider it successful?
- What do I need more of in my day?
- What do I need less of in my day?

Whatever you answer, don't forget to include time to play as well as time to work!

2. Incorporate the business into the family. One of the biggest mistakes that I made in my early career was trying to incorporate the family into the business rather than the business into the family. As I began to share this information with others, I discovered that I was not alone. Taking the time to get the family on board with your business is key to your business success. One of the most important strategies that you can implement into your business planning is to find out what is important to your family. Do they expect to have a full meal on the table every evening or would they prefer to spend an extra 30 minutes with you? Find out when you need to be in attendance at events and when you do not. One way to discover these answers is by having a family planning meeting once a week.

The most important business decision you will make is getting your priorities in the right order. This not only leads to a more successful business, but you will be less stressed so that you can enjoy all aspects of your life.

3. Give yourself the gift of NO. If you are honest with yourself, you will admit that more often than not, you put your personal needs last. As a result, you find yourself saying yes when you really want to say no. Unfortunately, when you continue to say yes, it keeps you from accomplishing the things that you really want and need to do to manage your life as a direct selling superstar. Creating a list of what matters most to you, establishing goals for your business and your personal life and setting your priorities are perfect strategies that will empower you as you decide to answer yes or no. Your priority list will be your guide in your decision making as you encounter everyday opportunities. By basing your choices on this list and implementing the word "no" into your time management system, you will soon realize that the word "no" is one of the most powerful tools that you can use. To help you define when to say yes and when to say no, ask yourself these questions:

- Will choosing to say yes add to my life or create more stress?
- Will choosing to say yes move me forward to achieving my goals?
- If I say yes, what is the cost—emotionally and physically—to me, to my family, to my business?
- Is it something that will improve my career and life-balance, make me feel better or benefit my family, or will it keep me from achieving my goals?

Make Plans to be a Direct Selling Superstar

Being a direct selling superstar isn't something that just happens or, as some might think, just a matter of luck. It requires establishing personal business habits, pinpointing personal and team expectations and continuous goal setting in all areas of your life—all while you are striving to be the best that you can be. The ultimate strategy to incorporate that will ensure you stay focused, organized and on course is having routine planning sessions.

There are three planning sessions to consider:

1. **Monthly planning.** An overview of the next month, including your monthly expectations and goals, a listing of anything and everything that you want or need to do to secure these expectations and ensure that your goals will be accomplished, and any appointments and

events—personal, family and business—that you already have confirmed.

2. Weekly planning. A time to tweak your week and make sure that all elements of your life puzzle pieces are included based on your values and priorities.

3. Daily planning. Take time every day to make plans for an ideal day. Some people choose to do this in the evening before they go to bed; others choose the first thing in the morning. Most importantly, find the best time for you. To make sure that you stay focused, maximize the time that you have in your day and determine your daily priorities, ask yourself these questions:

• What do I absolutely have to get completed today?
• Is there anything that I have been procrastinating about?
• What will move me forward to achieving my goals today?

Based on your answers to these questions, prepare your "to do" list for the day. I suggest that you choose only three things that you most want or need to accomplish and that you are convinced will have the biggest impact on your day and your goals. Next, decide how long each of these tasks will take and assign them a time to be started and completed.

Every evening take a few minutes to review your day. What was the best thing that happened? What could you improve? What will you do differently or say no or yes to in the future?

Celebrate

Every day we are presented with opportunities that have an impact on how we live our lives and the accomplishments that we enjoy. Every accomplishment—large or small—deserves a celebration. It is a misconception that you should only celebrate the big things in life. I encourage you to find a reason every day to celebrate life. Celebrate you. Remember, "Life happens on a daily basis." On occasion, your day might not go as planned. But when you take the time to distinguish your values and priorities and know and understand that ultimately the choices that you make based on that information determine the results of your day, you will find yourself more in control of your time, your life and your business.

Make a commitment to yourself to make daily choices that empower you and make it possible for you to say, "If I had today to live all over again, I would do it the exact same way!"

MARTHA STALEY, CDC
Speaker and Direct Selling Trainer
Your Perfect World®

Your perfect day, your way... everyday!

(618) 569-5655
martha@yourperfectworld.net
www.yourperfectworld.net
www.marthastaley.net

A direct sales professional for over twenty years, Martha Staley has been a top leader growing a multi-million dollar organization and has earned top awards for sales, sponsoring and leadership. Her passion is to empower every woman to live the life of her dreams—not just some days but every day. She believes that you have the power to create your own unique world based on your personal values, priorities and the realities of your ever-changing life and circumstances.

Martha's programs focus on identifying and taking on the obstacles in life that can keep you from achieving your business and personal goals. She possesses the unique background and credentials to help you overcome challenges through personalized programs and make them the blueprint for your business and your life each and every day.

Martha is the Founder and CEO of Your Perfect World®, a Certified Dream Coach®, speaker and direct sales trainer. She is a member of the distinguished International Coach Federation (ICF), The National Association of Professional Women (NAPW), Direct Selling Women's Alliance (DSWA), a Certified Elite Leader and a contributor in the DSWA's *Mentored by the Masters* program.

An Organized Office
Systems for Sanity

By Anne Nelson

"Organizing is what you do before you do something, so that when you do it, it is not all mixed up."
—Christopher Robin, in Winnie the Pooh by A. A. Milne

Clutter and office disarray are emotionally draining. Think about how you feel when you walk into your office. What is the first thing that comes to mind? Is it, "I can't wait to connect with my consultants today." Or do you sigh, "Where do I even begin?" The more chaos in your office, the more your productivity plummets and your focus wavers. Those piles scream "red flag" about all that unfinished business. The Post-it® notes remind you that you need to call consultants and customers. The orders and products spread around the office leave you thinking about the sales you need to get or the hostesses you need to coach. The stack of mail reminds you that you still need to pay bills and register for convention. There are so many interruptions to your thinking when there is clutter in your office that you can become paralyzed about where to start, or find yourself completely stressed because you are always behind in what you want to accomplish.

Creating an organized office so you can be productive and feel empowered will positively affect the steps you take to grow your business. There are many areas in your business where organization and systems can make your life easier. The key is to review all those areas, learn tactics and tools for change, and then choose the areas that are easy to maintain and critical to your success. Whether it's managing a profitable sales business, or keeping up with a growing team, creating an organization plan customized to you will make a difference in how you feel about your business, how others perceive your business, and more importantly, you will be able to put your energy where you function best.

Get Your Office in Order

The first step in developing systems is to begin with how your office is organized. Schedule time on your calendar when you will once and for all get rid of piles, notes, stacks of stuff and all the clutter. Consider the day you overhaul your office as a personal retreat, bringing clarity to the direction in which you want your business to go. Make a commitment to yourself that you will not compromise that time.

> *"Begin at the beginning,"* the King said gravely, *"and go till you come to the end; then stop."*
> —Alice's Adventures in Wonderland by Lewis Carroll

To get yourself out of overwhelm, start organizing by getting all the piles off your desk. A simple method is to lay a row of colored sheets of paper on the floor, labeled with categories into which you will sort the papers from piles. At the end of the row is a paper labeled for recycling and one for shredding. Start with a stack of papers from your desk and sort each one onto a categorized pile. When you are finished sorting out your piles, place the colored paper with the category title on the top of the stack, clip them all together and stack them in a to-do basket for your assistant. She can be the one to label all the file folders, put the stacks in appropriate files, take out the recycling and shred the papers you don't need. If you do not have an assistant, consider getting one. Even a few hours of support every week will help keep you organized, and your assistant can do those tasks that are not the best use of your time.

Some piles may require actions such as following up with an order or replying to phone messages. Sort those in order of importance and put them in your own to-do file. Schedule time every morning to work specifically on the tasks from your to-do file before you even open your email. Make it a commitment to whittle your file down an hour a day or schedule a couple blocks of time each week and get it all done. The time it takes you to do this will literally save you hours of time and eliminate frustration when you can't find what you are looking for.

If you have papers that have been sitting on your desk, on the floor next to your desk or piled for months on the bookcase, chances are pretty high you are not going to need them for several more months— if at all. So sort through them and start recycling that paper. Conquer the clutter in one day and you'll feel energized and in control so you can take the next steps to creating systems that enable you to stay focused and productive.

Create Boundaries to Successfully Blend Business and Home

I quickly discovered it was an interruption to my family life when I would answer the phone every time it rang just in case it was a customer or consultant. You want to be conscious of the message you send to your family when you allow calls to interrupt your time with them. The flip side is true, too; what message are you sending to your customers and consultants when you can't be reached or you stop a conversation with them to respond to a child? Having a separate phone line for business is a very simple and easy way to separate your business from your private life.

Your personal home life, be it single, married, single parent or caretaker of an elderly parent, can seriously impact what boundaries will be best for your business. Theories abound about whether or not you need to have office hours. The only right answer to that lies in the answer to the question, "Is what you are doing now working for you?" If it is, you're set. If not, make changes until you find what works for you.

If you often think about your family when you are working, or think about your business when you are with your family, you may want to reconsider when it is best for you to work and when it is best for you to play. When my children were really small, I set my office hours around their nap times or school schedule. As our family expanded and the children grew into teenagers, the schedule shifted again. Other concerns include what you want from your business for your family and how much time it will take to accomplish that. Given what you want and need for your family, you can determine how much time to put into your business and when the most appropriate time to work will be. The key is to block those times off on your calendar and honor them. One beauty of your direct selling business is you are the owner and you can feel free to work it as it best fits you.

Establish Workable Business Routines

Routines help you stay organized and on top of your business so your business doesn't run you. Try some of these suggestions to create effective routines.

- Serve a simple dinner on the night of a party or team meeting.
- Work the same days each week to create consistency in both your business and your family life.
- When you book a party, schedule the hostess coaching call in your date planner at the same time.

- Schedule time the day after your party to make follow-up calls.
- Make your follow-up calls to prospects before you place an order.
- Keep your personal products separate from your party samples so they are always ready to go and you don't forget key items.
- As a leader, keep a portable box packed with everything you always take to team meetings to avoid that last-minute rush or panic.

Add a Portable Office

For the fourteen years I was in the field I kept my consultant business in a portable hanging file box. Even when I was a leader, I kept my consultant business in the same portable box to keep it separate from my leadership responsibilities. It is an easy way to keep all your supplies organized and together so you can take it and go anywhere. For consultants without office space at home, this "business in a box" is ideal. In the portable box you store hostess coaching packet supplies, files for order forms, promotional flyers, pending orders, orders received, catalogs and recruiting brochures, as well as thank you note cards, stamps and any paperwork you need.

Once you find yourself with an organized office and you have routines in place for your family, you are ready to dive into the systems that allow you to function with any size team efficiently and effectively.

> *"There can be no one best way of organizing a business."*
> —Joanne Woodward, American actress

Using Binders, Files and Computer Programs Effectively

Take a deep breath here and relax. There is not one right way to manage your responsibilities. What is important is that you find the system that works for you. You may be a very visual person and what works best for you is a binder system where you can quickly see which binder you need, grab it and go. You may function best when there is nothing in sight to distract you and a file system in a drawer is the best solution for you. You may be very technically savvy and can't imagine not using computer programs for your calendar, your files and your customer and consultant tracking. Ultimately, you want a system you can use with ease, which may be a combination of binders, files and your computer programs.

Regardless of which system you put into place, there are some categories which need to stay organized for you to reference for future planning, training and tracking team growth. Company newsletters, promotions, team incentives, activity reports and training notes can all be kept in binders. Customer service, prospects and consultants can easily be tracked and managed in binders as well, especially if you are not comfortable with computer programs. If your company uses a weekly or monthly review form, you may want to record those results in an Excel® spreadsheet so you can easily sort achievements and milestones for recognition. If your company offers software that does this for you, there's no need to reinvent the wheel—use the company program.

Tracking Guides

There are a number of tracking guides you can put into place to help manage every aspect of business from the data from corporate office and your team to customer tracking and the progress new recruits are making in their business. Though there are others, here are a few with which you can start.

New consultant tracking. Getting a new consultant off to a successful start in her first 90 days will result in greater retention. You can help make sure she doesn't miss a step by tracking the actions she needs to complete in her first 90 days. This can be done in a spreadsheet or on a tracking grid printed out and kept in a New Consultants binder. List each new consultant down the left column with her start date in the next column. Additional columns to add can include: kit purchased, date of kick off, date quick start completed, attended first meeting, new consultant training, first sponsorship and so on based on the company-suggested activities for a consultant's first 90 days in the business.

Tracking consultant connection calls. Staying in touch on the phone is one way you stay personally connected to your team. Divide your team into three categories based on how frequently they need to hear from you and enter their names on the designated tracking chart. If you are a visual person with a really large team, instead of using a computer spreadsheet or a tracking form in a binder, pick up poster-size tracking charts from a teacher's store. Each time you make a connected call, enter the date on the chart. You can see at a glance who you speak to frequently and who you do not contact often enough.

Tracking consultant coaching calls. The support you provide to your business builders and leaders to help them reach their sales and sponsoring goals is invaluable. If you want to be effective in assisting them, record the date, length of call, brief overview of the content discussed, options generated and accountable actions in a binder or in a computer file. When you keep this information in one area, you can see at a glance when you have a consultant who is slipping away from her goals or facing the same challenge week after week. With this information in front of you, you can better train and coach her to take the right steps and evaluate how to improve her actions toward reaching her goals.

Try It and Tweak It

The benefits of establishing systems are many:

- You can pass on some tracking responsibilities to an assistant and know if she is out of the office you can still find the information you need.

- You have laid a good foundation for your leaders who promote out so that they are able to duplicate what you do.
- You can spot consultants who need your help to stay on track.
- You are better able to support new consultants in their first 90 days.
- You know what to expect, where to find information and you are in control of what is happening in your business.

Ask yourself what would make the biggest impact on your sanity and start there. Is it organizing the piles strewn all over your office? Maybe it's declaring when you will work your business and when you'll close the office doors for family time. You don't have to commit to every system here. Implement a few on a trial basis. If one doesn't work, try another approach and tweak it to work for you.

A good place to start would be with a couple of tracking systems using binders. Pick one to start with today and keep your focus on it for a few weeks. Then come back, reread this chapter and select the next systems you want to create. Recognize your systems may evolve as your team grows, teams promote out, company training changes, or you become more comfortable with new organizing concepts.

One of the greatest rewards of having workable systems will be when you watch your productivity soar and see your goals realized, raising the joy factor in your business as you lose the stress of chaos.

Make sure you read Martha Staley's chapter in this book, *Managing Life as a Direct Selling Superstar* that starts on page 47. Her chapter is filled with valuable information that directly relates to everything I've touched on in this chapter.

ANNE NELSON
Joy Zone, LLC

Raise the joy factor into your direct sales business!

(605) 271-9663
anne@yourjoyzone.com
www.yourjoyzone.com

Like night vision goggles for those dark corners of business, Anne's practical solutions bring out the *"Aha!"* in consultants, eliminating fear-induced setbacks and excuse-preventing actions. An expert in direct sales, she lightens the path to building a positive, productive business. Anne inspires consultants to dream big, take action and get results using simple, proven, use-it-today strategies and systems. With her tell-it-like-it-is style, audiences are captivated by her honest and humorous real life stories and insights that leave them jazzed, joy-filled and ready to soar.

She is the author of *Find Your Joy Zone* and *Inspiring Incentives*, and the creator of the Master Business Series CDs, all available through www. YourJoyZone.com. In addition to being an author and speaker, Anne specializes in training and consulting for start-up companies and is a DSWA Certified Coach for leaders committed to expansion and growth. Anne's passion and personal mission is to empower women to reach beyond self-set limits to create prosperity, abundance and joy in life. Partner with Anne Nelson for your next event!

Run Your Business Like a Business
So It Will Pay You Like a Business

By Rhonda Johnson

"How you do anything is how you do everything."
—T. Harv Eker, leadership expert, speaker and author

Operating a home-based business can give you the best of both worlds. Like all small business owners, you enjoy the satisfaction of being your own boss and the person who makes the decisions. In theory, you can run a successful business out of your home and have the flexibility to be there for your family, spending more time with your children and arranging your work commitments around your family's needs. You can also enjoy the benefits of some very generous tax advantages.

Whether you are just getting started in your direct selling career or you have an established business, there are several good reasons to run your enterprise as a business:
- You can know from day one whether or not you are making a profit and how much it is.
- You can see how profitable your business is now, not months later, so you can make intelligent decisions about all of the facets of operating your business.

- You can maximize your tax deductions so that you keep more of that profit.
- You will be prepared—not crazed—around tax day by having systems set up to keep track of your income and deductible expenses.

Make a Plan and then Work Your Plan

Creating a business plan for your direct selling business can be a very useful exercise, whether you are just starting or have been working your direct sales business for years. Working through a business plan will fill in the gaps in your knowledge and provide details of how you are going to do what needs to be done to start and run your business successfully. This plan becomes the blueprint for your direct sales success. Writing a business plan can be time consuming, but it is essential if you want to have a successful business that is going to survive. The process of writing a business plan can do wonders to clarify where you have been and where you are going.

Write it down. The most important purpose of a business plan is to transfer your business dreams and vision onto paper so that you can produce it in the real world. This is more important than you might think. There are many people who dream, but very few who can turn their dreams into reality. You have a better chance of accomplishing your goals when they are written down.

Set achievable goals. This is easier than it sounds. Sit down with your upline or mentor and, based on the retail profit and compensation plan of the company you are with, set short-term income goals for yourself. If your immediate goal is $500 per month, then how many parties, working with the company average per party, does it take for you to achieve your goal? How many dollars of product do you need to sell to achieve a monthly income of $500? If your company has more of a network marketing structure, figure out how much team volume you need to reach your monthly financial goal.

Keep your business plan simple and make the goals attainable for the amount of time you have to work your business. Working through a business plan will fill in the gaps in your knowledge and provide details of how you are going to do what needs to be done to start and run your business successfully. This plan then becomes the blueprint for your ongoing direct sales success. For more about goal setting, see Martha Staley's chapter, *Managing Life as a Direct Selling Superstar* on page 47.

Delineate your business activities. One of the best things about direct selling is that you can work your business anywhere and anytime. Take a look at how you spend your day under "normal" circumstances, and note all of the occasions where you come in contact with other people. Having a home-based direct selling business means that you may be able to convert these occasions to business-building activities.

Immediate Cash Benefits

Outside of generating actual sales or getting those bonus/commission checks, there are substantial immediate cash benefits available to you through tax deductions from your business.

"From your front door" deductions. As outlined in your business plan, you may promote your business anywhere, every day. With a little planning and by proper documentation, a high percentage of the use of your personal vehicle can be deductible. For a 20,000 mile per year business usage vehicle, this amounts to over $10,000 in tax deductions for your business each and every year.

Hire your children. You can now hire your children between the ages of 6 and 17 to work for your business, and convert the former expense of their allowances to tax deductible wages without paying any payroll taxes. Current tax law allows you to pay each of them up to approximately $5,700—tax-free to them and deductible to you—as wages for helping you in your business. For a family with two to three children, this deduction alone can be worth from $8,800 to $13,200 in tax deductions, all because you are now in business for yourself, with your family!

Write off your home. Even the cost of your home itself becomes legally deductible through the depreciation now available to you based on the percentage of your home used for business. In addition, most sole proprietors may take deductions of other home expenses, up to the extent of the net income of your home business, such as the use of your home while making product and sales presentations, sales meetings, sales trainings, communication, administration, or the display and inventory of products and samples used to generate sales and profits in your business.

Give yourself a raise. Having a home-based business with a profit motive qualifies you for additional tax deductions. As a result you will be paying less tax and keeping more of what you make. If you have a regular job where you are an employee, give yourself an immediate raise by reducing your withholding. Fill out a new W-4 at work. By increasing your allowances, your take-home pay will increase starting with your next paycheck. This step can make all the difference by giving you the extra cash you need to finance your new venture. What you are doing is getting the additional refund for which your home business qualifies you in each paycheck rather than waiting until you file your tax return next year.

How the IRS Views Your New Business

The IRS anticipates that you have chosen to be an entrepreneur because you have already researched and understand the expectations involved. Did anyone ever tell you before you started sharing your new direct sales adventure with friends and family that there was a business side to this commitment? Would that information have stopped you from continuing with your decision? Recordkeeping and taxes are enough to cause concern for even the bravest of individuals. Here are the key areas to focus on so that you are in the best position possible when it comes to dealing with the Internal Revenue Service—and your state taxing authority as well.

Profit motive. The IRS requires that you have the intent to make a profit. If you were to get into an audit situation the following items are how they evaluate your business integrity:

1. Are you working your direct selling business in a businesslike manner, maintaining complete and accurate books and records?

2. Does the time and effort you put into direct selling indicate that you intend to make a profit?

3. Are you depending on the income from your business as your only income?

4. If you are claiming losses, are they a result of circumstances beyond your control or are they normal business start-up expenses?

5. Have you changed methods or even companies in an attempt to improve profitability?

6. Do you or your business associates have the knowledge needed to establish a successful direct selling business?

7. Have you been successful in making a profit in similar activities in the past?

Setting Up Your Home-Based Business

Keep good records. Your records must be permanent, accurate and complete, as well as clearly establishing your income, deductions and credits. This is the least interesting or desirable activity for most business people. Some of you would rather go to the dentist than do any consistent record keeping. The thought of paperwork and taxes is enough to make you lose sleep. So let me suggest that you find a recordkeeping system that will work for you. Regardless of the cost, if the system you choose is one that takes too much effort and you do nothing—it is worthless and a total waste of time and money. On the other hand, don't allow your legitimate deductions to be disallowed because you can't prove them because you have not kept careful records.

Make sure you have all the necessary documentation. Your business success is reflected in the quality of your documentation. Appointment books and calendars are an important part of the materials you need to maintain and keep year to year. Notations on appropriate dates can provide backup information for things such as business mileage, meal expenses, parking fees and business trips. In fact, if you're traveling at all for business, it's a good idea to record in your appointment book what activities you did each day you were away. This can be helpful if you ever need to prove that it was really a business trip. You need to be prepared to supply the IRS with documentation on how you spent your money by keeping receipts, canceled checks and charge card/ debit card slips.

Find a system. We all need to find systems that work for us. Buy it, and then consider hiring a person to implement it for you, or outsourcing your recordkeeping and bookkeeping so you have the time needed to grow your business. I never recommend a new business owner purchase and learn new software. That activity immediately causes you to put time and energy into the business, rather than spending your time establishing and working the business. It is especially important in the beginning to be spending as much time as possible on the activities that generate income. It can be easy to get caught up in keeping track of your business finances. When we fall into that trap, we often confuse activity with accomplishment, and then wonder why we don't have more sales. Hire a bookkeeping and tax expert so you do not have to become one. This is not a good use of your time.

Use your time wisely. If you insist on doing your own bookkeeping, then tackle that project during non-business hours. I typically recommend systems that are easy to learn such as Expense Tracker® or Tax Tools Pro®. Expense Tracker is a fun and ridiculously easy-to-use money tracking system that can be your secret to enjoying more financial freedom than you ever thought possible. The truth is that you must track your spending in order to control it. Tax Tools Pro is already set up for a home business and painlessly guides you through the steps to claim every one of the home-based business tax deductions allowed. I never recommend QuickBooks® unless that is a system with which you are already familiar.

Have designated business credit card and checking accounts. Strive to always use business account checks and credit cards for your purchases—not cash. Designate a credit card and a bank account that will be used only for your business. Once again, the key word is "designated." A card with minimal activity can be used as long as you do not commingle personal and business expenses. The same goes for having a separate checking account for your business that ideally has a debit card connected to it so you can actually access money in your account without running up a credit card balance.

Commingling your personal and business income and expenses is anything but a professional business practice. The decision whether an expense is business or personal needs to be done at the time of purchase—not after the purchase is complete. Yes, this means if you are shopping and part of your purchases are for your business use and some for personal, you need to divide the items and have two transactions.

Set up your home office. An office can be a room or a portion of a room, like the corner of a bedroom or a section of the kitchen counter. Determining the square footage of this area assists your preparer in determining the percent of business use expenses that you can deduct.

Get Professional Help with Your Bookkeeping and Tax Returns

When choosing the method of recordkeeping you also need to keep in mind what you will need to give to your tax preparer. Taxes are one of the greatest reasons to have a business. Keeping your books at a professional level during the year can help to alleviate stress as April 15th approaches. With a business, your tax situation can be pretty complex. You need specialized advice and tips. Your goal should be to pay as little taxes as possible.

Taxes should always be considered an ongoing process—not an event. If you are dragging out your box of receipts on April 10th hoping to meet the deadline, you are most likely not in control of your business financial destiny. The primary reason people overpay their taxes is a lack of good record keeping. How can you possibly track deductions that you aren't even aware of? Are you one of those business owners that are giving the IRS a big tip—basically paying more than your share? Remember: treat your business like a business and it will pay you like a business.

Interview prospective preparers. Before choosing a tax preparer, always interview them. Ask these questions in order to select the right tax professional for you:

• **What licenses or designations do you have?** EAs (Enrolled Agents) are my personal favorites because their sixteen-hour exam is all on taxes. Approach the "retail corner" preparers with caution. Their testing and experience is often very limited. CPAs are typically very expensive and extremely limited in their understanding of the tax rules for home businesses. The testing they take is typically sixteen hours, but with only four on taxes. You can find some that have additional education and embrace the tax benefits for the business from home. However, you need to complete this interview process before you decide.

- **How long have you been actively preparing taxes?**
- **In what tax issues do you specialize?** You are hoping to find someone that primarily prepares for small businesses, Schedule C businesses, partnerships, LLCs, S-Corporations and C-Corporations.
- **How long, approximately, will it take to finish my return?** Three days is usually adequate. Be cautious of the ones that prepare the return while you talk to them. A good preparer needs time to input the information and evaluate your return for the best possible outcome.
- **With what direct selling businesses are you familiar?** You should recognize some of the companies.
- **What is your opinion of direct sales?** A good preparer understands that employees get to write off almost nothing, but a business gets to write off almost everything. These aren't new rules. They were established in 1913 when Congress created the two-tax system: one system for employees and the second for employers. The business tax system received preferential treatment. It hasn't changed. This refers to Schedule C and Schedule 8829 home office forms.
- **Are you familiar with the "exclusive use" rule?** The "exclusive use" rule question is the fastest way to determine if your preparer actually respects the profession and is familiar with the taxes. The rule is simple. If you are participating with a product-based company and have product inventory and/or product samples in your residence as your sole fixed business location, you avoid the need to maintain part of your home for the exclusive use of your business.

Have Your Business Pay You Like a Business

No one can think themselves to success. However, everyone can climb the ladder one step at a time. You choose the ladder. Is it sturdy enough? Is it long enough? Is it placed correctly? Success is not achieved by avoiding risk; it is achieved by overcoming risk. Be positive, but realistic. In short, run your business like a business so it will pay you like a business. After all, isn't that why you made the decision to have a business? Apply what we have discussed here and watch your business flourish.

RHONDA JOHNSON
Accountable Solutions

We are making tax a game...let's play to win!

(866) 282-3127
rhonda@rhondakjohnson.com
www.makingtaxagame.com

Rhonda is a uniquely qualified tax specialist. She is Managing Partner of Accountable Solutions, a full-service accounting firm she started 20 years ago, and one of the fastest growing firms serving direct sellers. Rhonda has 34 years of direct sales experience, over 20 years as a business owner and 9 years as a national speaker and author. As Director of the Prosperity Center for DSWA, the Direct Selling Women's Alliance, she has helped coach consultants in over 160 different direct sales companies.

She has written three books, including the bestselling *Making Tax A Game* with Tom Bass, published by Accountable Solutions in 2008. Her latest undertaking is as Director of Tax Strategies for The Expense Tracker, an international firm created to provide businesses, large and small with the tools needed to succeed.

Featured as a keynote speaker at numerous national events, Rhonda captivates audiences with her enthusiasm. Her well-researched, high-energy presentations are delivered in a down-to-earth style that reaches everyone.

She is dedicated to inspiring and motivating entrepreneurs to take control of their finances and feel valued for the profession they have chosen. Rhonda believes in paying your fair share of taxes—just not leaving a tip.

Partner Up for
Greater Direct Selling Success

By Kimberley Borgens, CBC

Imagine going through life without anyone cheering you on, telling you that you can accomplish something, overall having to be the only one who ever does anything to support you. What if you never have someone to hold you accountable to what you say you want to achieve, or letting you know that you are not doing your best and encouraging you to step it up. That kind of life may be lonely, sad and disappointing.

In my life as a coach and entrepreneur I have found that I am much more successful when I have somebody walking beside me on my success journey. Having an accountability partner has helped me to stay on track even if only to prove to my partner that I could do it. When I am challenged, knowing someone is on my side to make it through all the obstacles is very comforting. That is what I want for you as you pursue your direct selling goals.

What do scuba divers, commercial airplane pilots and most successful team leaders have in common? They have a buddy in place. A scuba diver has a partner check her oxygen tank before going down into the ocean. Commercial airplane pilots have a copilot to keep them on track. Successful team leaders often have someone to hold them accountable for reaching the goals they desire to achieve. The reason they have an accountability partner is not because they aren't capable, knowledgeable or powerful enough to do it themselves—it is because they know success is much more rewarding when someone is watching their back. Life offers up many distractions, and having a partner to check the details adds that extra bit of safety and security from being dragged down by the challenges in life.

I live close to San Francisco where they have some of the best Dungeness crab. I spoke to some of the restaurateurs on Fisherman's Wharf who have all shared this same story with me. When you put a lot of crabs in a pot to boil, as the water gets warmer all the crabs start working hard to get out of the pot. When a crab is getting close to getting out of the pot, what happens is that the other crabs below begin to pull the first one back into the pot. Every one of the crabs is fighting for itself to get out of the pot. Thus no crabs ever get out of the pot. They fight to pull the other crabs down and no one survives. People often behave this way. When they see others being more successful they start pulling on them to try to catch up and end up bringing everyone down in the process. Having an accountability partner helps push you up over the edge and then you can reach down and pull them out, too.

> *"Lots of people want to ride with you in the limo,*
> *but what you want is someone who will take the bus with you*
> *when the limo breaks down."*
> —Oprah Winfrey, American media icon

As an entrepreneur in direct selling, you are responsible for making your business successful. You are your marketing department, the salesperson, the customer service supervisor, the team recruiter and the sales associate, as well as all the other business hats you fill. You may also be wearing the hats of wife, mother, friend and sibling—just to name a few. To keep it all straight in life, we often have friends we can call when things get tough. You want to have an accountability partner in business for the same reason. Your partner may be an old friend, a new friend, an acquaintance from a distance or just someone you see as successful. You may come to a point where you struggle to stay focused on what you started. Why not find someone to walk beside you in your direct selling business? An accountability partner can:

- Help keep you on track
- Provide you with accountability
- Monitor your progress
- Offer creative ideas
- Play the role of cheerleader as needed
- Play the role of drill sergeant as needed

A partner can inspire you with amazing ideas when you are experiencing a dry spell and there is a crunch to earn your next company-sponsored vacation, monetary incentive or award.

Success Starts with Enlisting the Right Accountability Partner

Look for someone who is motivated, has a positive attitude and:

- Is in the same direct sales company as you, or in a different and complementary business going after the same target market as you
- Has a different personality style so that you can utilize each other's strengths
- Has similar interests and/or challenges as you

If you have been in business for awhile, you may want to find a partner who is just starting out. Sometimes, a new person will remind you to go back to the basics and you wind up taking your business to a higher level as a result.

Provide an opportunity for each partner to mentor the other in business. This can release some time for your leaders to find balance in their own businesses and not have to focus so much on training people. However you decide to choose an accountability partner, be sure that you both are willing to challenge each other's areas for improvement as much as you honor each other's strengths. Friends are great in our personal lives. However, if they do not own their own business, they may not be able to entirely relate to the challenges you face. Finding an accountability partner in business who understands and can walk alongside you in this journey will help elevate your level of business and expand your team.

> *"The value of a relationship is in direct proportion to the time that you invest in the relationship."*
> —Brian Tracy, author and speaker

Some Tools for Creating and Maintaining a Successful Accountability Partnership

Once you find a partner, decide:

- How often the two of you will connect. Once a day, a week or a month?
- How long you want this relationship to last. One month, six months or a year?
- What day and time will you connect with each other on a regular basis?
- How will you connect? In person, phone, Skype™ or email?
- Who calls whom? Same person or will you rotate periodically?
- What is your level of confidentiality with each other? What can and cannot be shared?
- What if your partner does not show up on the call or appointment?
- What needs to happen to get back in agreement with each other?
- Set a starting and ending date.

At the ending date you can look at the costs and benefits of continuing, reevaluate and choose to continue or not. If you decide to keep going, set a new starting and ending date. If you both decide not to go forward, let each other know how valuable they were in your journey and always honor what she has brought into your life.

You may decide you want to find a new accountability partner to get you to a riskier level, and as much as you honor your first partner, she may not be ready to take that bigger risk with you. There is no judgment in the choice—it is about making a powerful business decision and staying on that path to success. You can always stay connected and be friends. You may decide to connect her up with someone else on your team who could benefit from her.

Set specific and measurable goals for your business and share them with your accountability partner. Let her know what you want to be held accountable for, when you want to be held accountable for it and why that is important for you. Then honor your partner by holding her accountable the way she has asked you to hold her accountable. Setting clear expectations with your accountability partner will allow you to know exactly what the desired outcomes are for both of you.

Does your partner clearly understand why you are asking for her support? Is it clear how what she is doing will benefit her reaching her goal? Can she create the picture of what she wants to accomplish in a way that you can understand and dream it with her? If either of you are not sure how to create the picture, get a mentor, coach, upline leader or friend to help you put it all into perspective.

Be Committed to Your Accountability Partner's Success and to Your Success

Being committed to your accountability partner does not always mean you agree with her. It means you are both strong enough to ask the hard questions so you can each determine what is in her— and your—best interest. She may choose to do something you are not willing to do. Can you still be committed to her even if you do not agree with the risk she is taking? Can you leave out judgment and be willing to tell her that you do not agree with her choice and yet you are willing to be there if she falls while taking that risk?

Ask your accountability partner about her level of commitment to each of her goals and action items. Ask her to quantify, on a scale of one to ten, how committed she is to achieving her goal or task. Usually a nine or ten means she is likely to accomplish it. Anything less than that should prompt you to ask her what it will take to get her to a higher level of commitment. Set up challenges and friendly competitions for each of you to go after in your business, such as:

- Whoever gets ten solid bookings first will have bragging rights on the next leader's call
- Create a 24-hour booking blitz
- Challenge each other in a 48-hour recruiting blitz
- Highest show sales for the week/month/quarter
- Most lead-generating follow-up calls

Creating simple challenges can help keep you both motivated and committed to your goals. What other friendly competitions can you create?

In order for this accountability relationship to actually work, you must ask your partner what she wants to create in her business. Does she want more bookings, higher show sales, more leads, more recruits or is there an incentive trip she wants to earn? Asking her questions around her business goals will encourage her to stick to them. If you tell her what you want her to accomplish then you are just being the leader and not somebody walking alongside a partner. Practicing your coaching skills with your accountability partner will give you practice in coaching your downline in the future. For more about coaching recruits, see Sallie Meshell's chapter, *Turning New Recruits into Leaders*, starting on page 209.

Remember, you are in business for yourself, not by yourself. There are great coaches, mentors and accountability partners who are willing to support you in your success. Your job is to take the risk and ask for support.

Note to Team Leaders

As a team leader, you may consider developing an accountability system to partner up your downline leaders in order to encourage their personal and leadership growth. This could be a benefit for people joining your team, knowing that when they join with you, they are not alone. Having two new recruits teaming up and learning the ropes together could maximize your training and help build a strong team.

Ways to Keep Your Partnership Productive

There may be some obstacles that could keep this relationship from being productive. Here are some things to watch out for:

1. Recognize you both have a contribution to make. Sometimes, when people come together, one may have higher intellectual or mental capacity and may decide to stand and defend her position so strongly that the other partner does not feel they can add any value to the relationship. This can cause you and your partner to feel as though they don't have equal power in the relationship, and there may be a heavy price paid—of partners breaking away. Even if you know you are right, are you willing to listen to outside ideas and perspectives? This is key for a successful accountability partnership.

2. Do not be a critic. It is easy to be critical of the choices your accountability partner is making. One of my mentors always said that being a critic is the easiest job in the world. The critic can have an opinion without even taking any risk. Don't fall into the trap of being a critic to your partner. Instead, ask questions to understand

and clarify her choices, allowing her to see a better way to take action. Do not let your ego get in the way of your relationship.

3. Respect each other's beliefs. Having an accountability partner does not mean you get to change her beliefs. We all have beliefs that serve us now or have served us at one point in our lives. Having someone help us to see if a current belief is serving us or holding us back is beneficial. However, it is always her own choice to change her belief system. If someone shows her how the belief she has may be limiting her, she can decide to change that belief. If she does not see it, no matter how hard we try to get her to see it, she will not change it. This is where, as her partner, you can support her even if she does not yet see the benefit of changing. Allow her the space to see the impact of her limiting belief and be there for her in the process.

4. Keep it confidential. Confidentiality may be broken without realizing it. Setting a level of confidentiality can help keep this from becoming an obstacle. Sharing honest information with your accountability partner and trusting that she will not go out and share the ideas with others, calling them her own, is a risk many partners face. Make sure you give credit where credit is due and be clear with each other about sharing ideas outside of your partnership.

Whether you would like help with accountability, motivation or celebrating your business, having a partner can be a great resource for you. An accountability partner is a powerful tool for accomplishing the goals you set for your success. Building a business does not have to be hard. Finding easier tools to help you create success can make business much more rewarding.

It is time for you to get started. List three possible accountability partners for you and decide who will stretch you the most and call them today. Build a powerful relationship with your accountability partner and watch both of your goals be accomplished and your dreams reach new heights.

KIMBERLEY BORGENS, CBC
Be A Legacy
Coaching, Consulting and Mentoring

Don't wait to leave a legacy—
be one now and you will automatically leave one

(209) 993-7632
kimberley@bealegacy.com
www.bealegacy.com

Kimberley Borgens is an award-winning entrepreneur, business coach, coach trainer and speaker. She works with small business owners to challenge them to excellence, focusing on coaching direct selling and network marketing leaders to reach their goals and build on their personal and professional development. This is accomplished though discovering limiting beliefs, competing commitments and building confidence.

Kimberley has the ability to coach in a wide area and with a range of people. Some of her favorite coaching arenas include emerging direct sellers, start-up entrepreneurs, women in discovery and parents of adolescent children. Her coaching creates tangible results through accountability and compassion.

Kimberley is a direct selling coach trainer with Coach Excellence, the DSWA accredited coaching school. A former facilitator with a major character development company, she majored in Business Administration and Administration of Justice, and is a graduate of Leadership Stockton and Leadership Lodi.

Kimberley lives in California with her husband and four children. Her passion for people has given her the ability to coach clients in Uganda, Mexico, Australia, Canada, Korea and the United States. She is passionate about life and encourages others to live a life of fulfillment.

Building an Online Presence for Your Direct Sales Business
Six Solid Ways to Expand Your Reach

By Karen Clark

"When two people meet, a third world is created.
And with today's technology, that world can grow exponentially."
—Anthony Robbins, self-help/inspirational author and speaker

When I first brought my direct sales business online in late 1998, the Internet was very young and there were no guidelines for how to conduct business, grow your network or even how to advertise online. Over the years, I tried just about everything at least once. Through trial and error, and in pockets of time alongside my "real life" business, I was able to establish a presence online that stuck, not only for myself but also for my company. Now when a potential customer or consultant goes online to research us, they find more than 100,000 references to our company and products. Would you like to be able to reach a vast network of new connections like that?

Why You Need This
Even if Your Business Is Doing Great
Promoting a direct sales business online does not replace your home parties, person-to-person contact or phone calls. Nothing replaces

meeting and connecting with people in person, and that is tried and true because it works. Establishing an online presence is something you do after your offline business is taken care of—after your calendar is full. Since your efforts online do not typically pay off overnight, keep your focus on your offline business while building an online presence. Going online might feel like just one more thing to do. Here is why it is worth your time:

This is a new era. According to Internet World Stats (www.internet worldstats.com/stats.htm), as of June 30, 2009, 73.9 percent of all Americans used the Internet on a regular basis. This is nearly a 140 percent increase since the year 2000 and it continues to climb. People are using the Internet on a daily basis to shop, interact and research—and some of that can involve YOU! Prospective new consultants may look in the search engines for your name and company affiliation. A potential customer who is considering purchasing from your company may look online for what other customers have said about your company or your product. Paying attention to your online presence helps you ensure your clients find what they are looking for.

Building an online presence enables you to serve more people. Not only will you be able to expand your business to a new town or region, you can also use the resources online to enhance your customers' and team members' experiences with you and your company, building trust and loyalty.

Having an online presence is a reputation-builder as you become known as an expert in your market. This builds credibility, and your presence online shows that you are treating your business like a business. It also shows the world the kind of person you are, so people can decide whether to do business with you—or not.

It's a Parallel Universe!

Direct sales is a relationship business and in the online world, relationships are also key. Think of the Internet as parallel to a real life party. Some people are friends, some are acquaintances and many are people you have not yet met. You have the potential of meeting new people who may or may not be interested in what you have to offer, and they may have something you are interested in as well. Conduct yourself online as you would in real life, focusing on building relationships. This will guide you to being true to your own values and principles, and prevent you from getting caught up in the latest hype or trends.

When you are building your online presence, ask yourself, "Is this something I would say, do or be in real life?" Activities that focus on connecting with people in real ways to instill loyalty and trust, or that help you position yourself as an expert or dependable resource in the field, will always further your business more than hard selling— offline and on.

A Word About Company Policy

Before venturing out online, read your company's Internet marketing policies carefully. Using a "don't ask, don't tell" approach hurts the integrity of your company and those consultants who abide by the rules. Your company has determined how best to meet consultant and company needs regarding the Internet, and it is important to respect that. The information in this chapter can be adapted to most company policies in order to have an effective online business presence.

Getting Started Online

With all of the options available to us, thinking about where to begin is truly overwhelming. Even starting with just one activity in which you participate consistently can create a strong presence. There is no need to do it all and besides, your offline direct sales business comes first.

Below are six solid methods I have found effective in expanding my reach online. Start with one and spend some time participating regularly. Results may not show up for months or even years. Your business exposure on the Internet is cumulative, and the actions you take will build upon each other over time. Because of this, starting with one activity at a time, and remaining consistent over time, will breed results over time. Do not compare your efforts to others in the profession. Stay the course and the results will come in the way of increased reputation, loyalty and business.

Note: The **Suggested Resources** listed at the bottom of each section are tools that I currently have success using. Please read the terms of service for each website before participating.

1. Make search engines work for you. Search engine optimization (SEO) is the practice of doing, saying and posting things online that enable people to find you more easily on the search engines. This is done through the use of relevant keywords—terms people actually use to look for what you have to offer—and relevant linking within your site, as well as links pointing to your site.

Research keywords within your market and use them naturally when you post online. This helps the search engines recognize you as someone who delivers what people are searching for, which in turn helps your site show up toward the top of the search results. Relevant links to you on quality websites also prove to the search engines that you are popular and deserve to be shared.

The search engines' customers are happiest and return to that search engine when their search efforts find them exactly what they are looking for. It is your job to make sure the search engines find you.

Suggested Resources:
- **Cricket's Ethical Search Engine Optimization Class.** Free email-based course on basic do-it-yourself SEO. www.gnc-web-creations.com/seo-optimization.htm
- **Google® Adwords Keyword Research Tool.** Look up a term you think would be a good keyword and get suggestions on other relevant keywords or phrases based on popularity and competition. www.adwords.google.com/select/KeywordToolExternal

2. Blogging for business. Hosting a blog is an effective way to have an online presence whether or not you also have a website. Blogging allows you to easily create something that looks like a website but is in fact a fluid journal where you can share ideas, post articles and give advice. This establishes you as an expert on a topic relevant to your business. Blogging also allows you to use important keywords that will be picked up by the search engines. If your company allows it, include links to your company website, or at least to your contact information so that potential clients can get in touch.

In direct sales, blogging can be especially helpful with interaction and relationship-building. Your blog posts can include things like tips and tricks, related articles of interest, or product features and "how-to's" that are helpful to know. Your blog can become a resource for your real life customers who will subscribe to receive new posts regularly. Since search engines index blogs, you will find potential new customers and team members reading your blog and asking how they can get involved.

Participate in other blogs by commenting. This exposes you to a new audience and increases links back to your website or blog. As you read blogs, add your relevant thoughts in the comments field. It's best not to mention your company or overtly sell in blog comments. Simply include the link to your own blog or website. Those who are curious will click through to find out more about you.

Suggested Resources:

• **WordPress® Blogging Platform.** Create a free, non-commercial blog using easy templates and familiar formatting tools. www.en.wordpress.com/features

• **Google Blog Search.** Search blogs based on your target market or keywords, and determine which blogs to visit. Subscribe to a Blog Alert to be notified of new posts about your favorite topics. www.blogsearch.google.com

3. Participate in social media. Social media is also known as Web 2.0 because the first phase of the Internet was not truly interactive. The second phase has more of an emphasis on social interaction, sharing, participating and serving. Social media is ideal for those in direct sales since the very nature of our profession is to be social. Word-of-mouth and relationship-building comprise the foundation of our businesses. Websites like Facebook®, Twitter® and LinkedIn® are enabling people to interact and communicate online more than ever before.

Participating in social media sites enables you to reach a broad range of people. Stay-at-home mothers, urban professionals, seasoned retirees and everyone in between, are participating in these sites. People you meet through social media will visit your listed website or blog and become a source of referrals or business for you due to the trust and rapport established.

Remember to be interactive. After all, it is called social media! The majority of what you post should be commenting and/or replying to what others have said, or offering advice when asked. Social media is not the place to just advertise your business. It is for those who want to create real connections through being real and serving others.

Suggested Resources:
- **Seesmic.** This application enables you to view and post on both Facebook and Twitter easily, while following your favorite keywords. www.seesmic.com
- **Mashable Social Media Guide.** A collection of current information and articles about various social media tools. www.mashable.com

4. Forums and online communities. The interactive nature of and community-building inherent in this method are perfect for direct sales. Forums allow you to open a folder with a particular topic and ask for help, share ideas or respond to other people's messages. List your business information in your signature so that everyone reading your messages will see what you do.

Participate in communities of interest to you in your non-business life, as well as some that are business-related. Participate in discussions by either answering someone else's questions or asking your own. There are forums on every topic of interest imaginable. When you have your business information in your signature—set up according to the site's guidelines—your exposure can lead to new business. You never know when someone reading a particular forum is looking for the very thing you have to offer.

Suggested Resources:
- **Big Boards Forum Directory.** Search for forums, message boards and communities based on your area of interest. www.big-boards.com
- **Google Groups.** Find or create your own online community, participate in discussions, share resources and recommend others. www.groups.google.com

5. Go multi-sensory with audio and video. It is well known that when people use multiple senses in particular experiences, they tend to learn more, retain information longer and participate more fully. In the direct selling profession we know that when our customers can see our product in person, hear the information from their consultant, and watch it being used through a demonstration, they are far more likely to place an order or become a hostess or consultant. In establishing an online presence, we are able to create a similar effect through the use of audio and visual tools.

Recording a demonstration of your product, a training for your team or an explanation of your hostess benefits, serves as a multi-sensory experience for your audience, building trust and rapport in a more memorable way than a two-dimensional website email, or flyer. Use audio and video tools to share information and teach—not advertise—in order to build a following that can be a valuable source of referrals as your listeners and viewers begin to share your resources with their own networks.

Suggested Resources:
- **Audio Acrobat®**. Record audio and video easily, then publish online through your blog, website or email. www.audioacrobat.com
- **YouTube®**. The most popular video-sharing website whose powerful search feature will expose you to new people interested in your product or opportunity. www.youtube.com

6. Get noticed by online media. A growing trend in traditional media—radio, television and print—is to offer information online either instead of, or in addition to, their original formats. Being noticed by the media has always been an area where direct sellers can get exposure for free, but the methods are changing. Today, the media use online tools to seek out sources for their content. Take advantage of this trend by participating in discussions, sending in feedback, and commenting on articles within the media outlet websites. Include a link back to your blog, website or contact information.

An additional way to become known by online media is to participate in product-based reviews or gift guides that they may offer their visitors. Traditional media, as well as top bloggers and online news sources, offer these online. Participating may cost you the price of the product samples you send, while the return is quite valuable through written testimonials, exposure and instant credibility.

Suggested Resources:
- **HARO: Help A Reporter Out.** This email list sends queries twice a day from media reporters and bloggers looking for content and sources to interview or include in reviews or gift guides. www.helpareporter.com
- **Blogged.** Search here for "Consumer Product Reviews" and "Gift Guides" to find online websites to which you can submit your product samples. www.blogged.com

Finding the Time to Implement Your Online Presence

"The secret of getting ahead is getting started. The secret of getting started is breaking your complex overwhelming tasks into small manageable tasks, and then starting on the first one."
—Mark Twain, American humorist, author, and lecturer

Successful businesswomen have a list of daily, weekly and monthly tasks. Add one or more online presence tasks to your list, schedule them into your daily, weekly or monthly plan, and stick to the schedule. Whether it is ten minutes each morning and evening, thirty minutes once a week, or a couple of hours once a month—you can do this. Set a timer if that helps, and remember to schedule these tasks on a regular basis. Remember that an online presence builds over time through exposure and interaction. Since the Internet records and keeps everything, take your time. When it comes to online presence, slow and steady wins the race!

KAREN CLARK
My Business Presence

(707) 588-9290
karen@mybusinesspresence.com
www.mybusinesspresence.com

Karen Clark is an Executive National Director with Story Time Felts. She has been certified as an ELITE Leader through the Direct Selling Women's Alliance, and was also honored with their exclusive Spirit Award in 2008. Karen has been the President of the Sonoma Marin Chapter of the DSWA for three years and has been featured as an Online Presence expert in the DSWA's Mentored by the Masters CD series. Karen has eleven years of direct selling experience with her company and has appeared in *Step Into Success* and *The Home Business Connection* magazines, as well as *Top Sellers Tell*, a book highlighting successful home-based entrepreneurs.

Nothing replaces connecting with people in person or by phone, and as an experienced and active direct selling leader, Karen walks the walk as she sells, books, recruits and supports a team offline, while expanding her reach and service online. Karen enjoys teaching others exactly where, when and how to spend their precious time online to establish a presence, while remaining true to their principles and personal business.

Embrace Public Speaking to Grow Your Direct Selling Business

By Caterina Rando, MA, MCC

Public speaking creates visibility for you in your geographic area more than anything else—without you spending a dime. You will quickly become known as the jewelry lady, the anti-aging lady, the fashion/clothing lady or the home décor lady. This allows you to easily become known as the expert in your area. Plus you meet so many more people so much faster. Public speaking is a hundred times faster than networking. When you go networking, you meet only a few people. When you are the speaker, everybody meets you. You don't have one-on-one conversations with everybody, but everybody feels like they have met you and had a conversation with you. Using public speaking as a direct selling business development strategy allows you to introduce your products to new people and make special offers to them for booking a party or making a purchase. You will leave your house to go to a room where you know no one and return home with new hostesses, customers and maybe even some new team members. What could be better?

See Yourself as an Educator

Public speaking allows you to educate people about your area of focus—quick meals, scrapbooking, losing weight or fitness—in an open forum. People get to hear tips and ideas that they might not know about, or even if they do, they can use the reminders. For example, you might sell health care, skin care or wellness products. There is so much to know about all those things. If you sell clothing or accessories there are many tips and tricks you can demonstrate to an audience to get more out of their clothing or accessory budget.

A presentation gives you the opportunity to educate people as a group. Public speaking is a one-to-many format rather than a one-to-one format. If you are meeting people one by one, you can only connect with a certain number of people. When you can speak to everybody at the same time by giving a presentation, it can mean talking to thirty potential clients at once. Aren't those incredible odds? Do you think you will get some business from that? Absolutely. Public speaking helps you fill your sales pipeline with lots of new people that you would otherwise never have met.

Use Public Speaking to Build Your List

One mistake a lot of direct sellers make is that they do not focus on building their email list. Public speaking is an ideal way to build your list fast. Not everyone in your audience is interested in what you have to offer today. However, through your speech you have begun to build a relationship with them. By getting their permission at your presentation to stay in touch with them you continue to build that relationship through your email contacts. When they need what you have to offer they will call on you.

One direct selling coaching client does an email special every month. Every month she has anywhere from 6–12 people take advantage of her special. That is a few hundred dollars extra each month from a quick email. Note that this email goes out to 1200 people. You might think, "Wow, that's a big list." Yes it is, and if you're speaking to grow your business you can build your list a lot faster than by adding only your show guests, customers and hostesses.

Go Where Your Potential Customers Go

Ask yourself, where are your potential hostesses, recruits and customers gathered? To answer that question, you have to first know who are your ideal hostesses, customers and new team members. While almost anyone can benefit from your products, not everyone is knocking down your door to get them. There is a particular type of person that is most likely to be interested in what you have to offer. Determine who that person is by looking at who your best customers and hostesses are. For example, is she a mom with small children who loves to cook, or is she a woman over 50 interested in looking great, or is she a mom in your community between 25 and 55 who loves clothes? Well, if she's a mom in your community between 25 and 55, where do you find her? Maybe she's at the health clubs, maybe she's at the businesswomen's groups, maybe she's at church, or maybe she's volunteering for the American Heart Association. All of these organizations have regular speakers.

Many women start their own groups around a common interest and they get together regularly in their own community that they have created—and they love to have speakers. You could present at an informal group. It doesn't always have to be a formal organization. Go ahead now and decide: Who is your ideal customer, hostess and potential recruit, and where does she spend her time with other people?

Put a List Together

Make a list of the kinds of groups you want to contact. Ask yourself what kinds of associations your potential customers would belong to—athletic associations, parent associations, businesswomen's groups or neighborhood groups?

Once you have an idea about where you would like to speak, begin to ask your current customers and hostesses what groups they belong to, and ask them to provide you with an introduction to the group as a possible speaker. Also, check newspapers for meeting announcements and search the Internet for groups in your area that meet the criteria for the kind of group you are looking for.

Once you identify a group, go and look at the website, find out who is the program chair for the group and when they have their meetings. If there is no program chairperson listed, find out who is the meeting chairperson or talk to the president. Be aware that groups that are run by volunteers often change the leadership every year. This means it can take some calls and a little detective work to find the right person. Your best bet is always to find a personal contact who can point you in the right direction and also vouch for you as a speaker.

Put Together a Speaker Sheet

Before you contact groups, you need a speaker sheet. A speaker sheet is a PDF document that explains a little bit about you, your talks and has your beautiful picture on it.

Your speaker sheet should start with a benefit-focused title at the top of the page. Don't put your name at the top. You are probably not yet famous like Suze Orman or Oprah Winfrey, where your name alone is enough to capture attention. Instead, put the benefit of what you are going to talk about at the top of your speaker sheet; something like, "Make Meals Fast," or "Look Like a Fortune on a Budget," or "Make Your Home Look Like a Magazine Layout with Easy Decorating Secrets." Make sure that your title is benefit-focused. You could put two speaking topics—or even three—on there, but don't have more than three.

Underneath the title of a talk, include a few benefit-focused bullet points. You want to include what you will cover and the benefits of the content you will be presenting. For example, for a decorating talk a benefit might be learning how different colors impact your mood at home, or discovering how furniture placement in a room impacts how much people use a room, or gain understanding of how to use accessories to finish the look of a home.

Be sure to also include a brief biography of yourself. Mention your credentials that relate to your topic—they do not have to be academic. Being a mom is a credential, being an arts and crafts enthusiast is a credential, being interested in and studying health and fitness for ten years is a credential. Having worked with women for five years to show them how to better organize their kitchens and their homes is a credential. You and your enthusiasm are enough. You do not need letters after your name to be qualified to give a thirty-minute talk.

At the bottom of your speaker sheet put your contact information so people can easily reach you. Then turn your speaker sheet into a PDF file to send via email, post on your website, blog, Facebook page, etc.

Connect with Your Targeted Groups

Once you have your speaker sheet, send an email to the groups on your list and write something like this:

Dear _____,

I am thrilled to learn about the Mothers of Pre-Schoolers Association that meets in Linwood on Tuesdays. You are listed as the program chair on the website. I have a great program on (your topic) that would be very beneficial to your group's members. Please let me know if you're interested in having me deliver a presentation for one of your upcoming meetings. Attached is more information on me and my presentations for your review.

Sincerely,

Your Name

After you send the email you want to follow up the next day, preferably with a phone call. Send the email first, because you want them to see your speaker sheet and have an opportunity to read it before you call.

Once you speak for one group, if you do a good job, you'll have no shortage of requests. When you present, be sure to ask the audience, "If you know another group that would enjoy my presentation, please let me know. I would love to deliver my program for them."

Before You Say "Yes"

In the beginning, speak to as many groups as possible to get as much practice as possible. However, when a group asks you to speak, gather some information before you say yes. Ask the questions below and make sure you like the answers:

- What is the agenda for the meeting?
- Who else is on the agenda?
- How long do you want me to talk?
- What is the event location?
- What time of day is the talk?
- Who will be in the audience?
- How many people will be in the audience?

To Prepare for Your Talk, Provide the Right Information

When you agree to do a talk, send off your photo and a one-paragraph description of your presentation. Do not let the organization pick the title of your talk or write the description. You provide this information.

Get Informed Ahead of Time

When you are speaking to a group there are a lot of logistics to handle. It is important to handle as many of these things as possible before the event so you do not have any last-minute surprises. This is a marketing opportunity for you and you want it to be worth your time.

What to Ask to Be Well-Prepared for Your Speech

- Is there time for questions and answers afterwards?
- Can I have a table to display my business information or products?
- Who is my on-site contact person?
- Who will be introducing me? What is her contact info?
- How will the room be set up? What kind of seating arrangement will there be?
- Will you/can you have a microphone for me?
- Where do I park?
- Will you send me the meeting flyer and email announcement?

What to Do During Your Talk to Gain Clients

Be sure to provide value to your audience. No one should have to become a customer to gain value from your presentation. Whatever your business, put together a talk that is full of tips, resources and ideas.

Use Client Examples

Find ways to discuss what you do for your customers as a way of supporting the different points you are making. People remember stories more than anything else after hearing a speech. Craft a few stories that describe the benefits your customers have received by following your advice or using some of your products. Describe a situation in which a customer found herself, share what happened and the resulting benefit to the customer.

For example: *Sheila loved sending out birthday cards, but she had to stop because they just got too expensive. She attended one of our scrapbooking card-making workshops and learned several ways to make beautiful cards for pennies. Now she is known in her community as the lady who makes the beautiful birthday cards.*

When you share examples of how your customers use your products, it helps the audience members see themselves in your examples.

Handouts That Can Get You Clients

- Always have something to give to the audience when you speak. Audience members can forget you when you walk out the door if they do not have a part of you to take home with them.
- Make up a handout with the five or seven or ten tips you are covering in your talk. For example, "Seven Ways to Stay in Touch" or "Eight Different Ways to Tie One Scarf."
- Include a flyer on your upcoming show, party or workshop.
- Be sure to put your business name, address, website and phone number on the bottom of each sheet of paper you give your audience.

Use an Action Sheet to Capture Business

An action sheet is a handout that you create that asks audience members what action they are going to take now that they have heard your talk. Toward the end of your presentation, have everyone take out the action sheet that you have already distributed, and walk them through it, having them fill it out as you review it with them.

Make sure you include the following on your action sheet:
- List of three qualifying questions to help you determine if you should follow up with an individual, such as:
  - Would you be interested in finding out about the benefits of hosting a party with (your company)?
  - Would you be interested in finding out how you can earn an extra $500.00 a month with (your company)?
  - Would you be interested in finding out more about our products?
- Ask audience members for their email address and offer to send them your monthly ezine and specials.

To make sure everyone turns in their form, hold a drawing and give away one of your products or a book of interest to audience members.

Lastly, make a special offer for hostessing or purchasing—good only for a certain period of time—for everyone in your audience. Give each person a customized order form/coupon with the offer written on it. Also, if you can bring and sell your products, offer a discount for purchases made before the end of the event.

What to Do After Your Talk to Build Your Business

Be available after your talks to answer any questions and connect with people. If anyone expresses an interest in your products or services, talk with them while you are still in the room, or make a follow-up date. Always avoid phone tag. It is not a good business-building activity.

The same day as your presentation—or the next day—send everyone in the audience an email thanking them for attending your talk and again mentioning any product or hostess specials. Be sure to include a tip or two and a link to your website.

Also, in your follow-up email ask people for help connecting you to any groups that might need speakers, or referrals to people who might be interested in your products or services. In this email, be sure to let them know that they have been added to your list and can unsubscribe at any time.

Use the ideas shared here and soon you will find yourself in the front of meeting rooms presenting to seats full of potential hostesses, new customers and team members. You will not only grow your business, you will expand your network, build your confidence and have fun—all at little expense to you. Get started with public speaking to grow your business today. You will be so glad you did.

CATERINA RANDO, MA, MCC
Direct Sales Coach and Speaker

Create a thriving direct sales business

(415) 668-4535
cat@directsalescoaching.com
www.directsalescoaching.com

Caterina is committed to helping direct sellers succeed in business—and it shows. Through her content-rich website, and in her business-building telecourses, Caterina's passion, experience, direct selling savvy and business acumen consistently come through.

Caterina is always a top-rated professional speaker, and is an experienced coach working with entrepreneurs and direct sellers since 1993. She is the best-selling author of *Learn to Power Think*, published by Chronicle Books, as well as a contributing author for the two most popular books for direct sellers, *Build It BIG: 101 Secrets of Top Direct Selling Experts*, and *More Build It BIG: 101 Secrets of Top Direct Selling Experts*, published by Kaplan and Dearborn, respectively.

She has served as The Success Center Director for the Direct Selling Women's Alliance, and has been featured as an expert in several best-selling books, including *Get Clients Now*, *Get Slightly Famous* and *The Eleven Commandments of Wildly Successful Women*.

Caterina is a Master Certified Coach, the highest designation awarded by The International Coach Federation, and holds a Bachelor of Arts Degree in Organizational Behavior and a Master of Arts Degree in Life Transitions Counseling Psychology.

Build Your Business by Building Relationships

By Beth Jones-Schall

If you knew that doing one thing well would...
• Increase your sales, bookings and recruiting
• Eliminate phone phobia
• Create consistency in your business
• Reduce cancellations
• Build your business with integrity
...would you make time for it? Would you make it a priority? That one thing is relationship building. Intentionally, purposefully investing your time in your hostesses and customers is the key to building relationships, and therefore building your business.

It is not that you do not want to build a relationship with your hostesses and customers, but rather that you have probably not really thought about it before. If you have, you may think it means a huge time commitment in your busy schedule. The good news is, in this chapter you will discover the importance of relationship building along with easy, effective, time-conscious steps to make relationship building part of your daily actions.

Love 'em and Don't Leave 'em

Without knowing it, direct sellers have created an "anti-relationship building" habit of focusing on hostesses and guests the night of the show (love 'em) and then forgetting about them the next day by moving on to the next show (leave 'em). This damages the potential for relationships to grow. You may think you have not forgotten about your previous hostesses and customers, but if they have not heard from you on a regular basis, you "left 'em." I believe this has led many consultants to consider hostesses and customers "theirs," yet those same hostesses and customers would not consider the consultant "theirs."

If you want to build a more profitable and sustainable business, I encourage you to examine your business for evidence of "love 'em and leave 'em" habits:

- Do you regularly find yourself in booking slumps?
- Do you dread calling people because they do not remember you?
- Do you get regular recruit leads from your shows?
- Do people ask if you are "still selling that"?

If you answered yes to any of the above, you have evidence of the "love 'em and leave 'em" syndrome. Read on for the cure!

Relationships Create Referrals

Not only will you find that curing the "love 'em and leave 'em" habit is helpful as you build a more profitable and sustainable business, you will also find your referrals will grow as your friendships grow. Friends refer friends because they know them and trust them. Friends especially refer friends who are consistent and dependable, which your commitment to relationship building will demonstrate.

Later we will discuss how to create opportunities for referral conversations during hostess coaching, as well as during your shows. In addition, your hostesses and customers, as well as your friends and family can be a great source of referrals. A few steps to keep in mind as you invite referrals from family and friends when you are not at a show:

1. Let them know how helpful referrals are to your business.

2. Keep your family and friends up-to-date on your business so they can be "public relations agents" for you. Be certain they are among your best customers so they can easily testify from personal experience.

3. Equip your family and friends with your business cards and catalogs to share with others in their circles of influence. Ask them often who they have met or talked with recently about your business so you can follow up promptly.

4. Share your business as you chat with friends on Facebook®, See Karen Clark's chapter on *Building an Online Presence for your Direct Sales Business* on page 89 for more details on how to use social media for networking.

5. Remember the adage, "To have a friend, you must be a friend." Consider that in the context of referrals: "To get referrals, you must give referrals." Be a resource for sharing referrals with others, from a great manicurist to a wonderful caterer. Be sure to ask others how you can help them through referrals. As you become a referral resource for them, they will become a referral resource for you.

Referrals that are prompted through the friendships and relationships you build will serve to sustain and build your business way beyond your show contacts.

Hostess Relationship Building

Now that you have discovered the value of building your business through referrals when you are not at a show, let us get down to the business of how to build relationships with your hostesses and customers. Here are the key steps to building a profitable, sustainable business.

Begin the process by building a relationship with your hostesses, since you have the opportunity to spend more time with them. Focus on being intentional and purposeful with each contact you make. The following is a hostess coaching process that focuses on building relationships, friendships and fun.

1. Before the Show

What matters to her matters to you. For most hostesses, the number one concern is attendance. So, that is your number one focus. The steps that will help increase show attendance and reduce cancellations include:

- **Providing guest list suggestions** of whom to invite, including friends, relatives, acquaintances, neighbors, kids' associations, church affiliations and people from school or work. These categories will help her expand her guest list to 30-40 guests.
- **Setting a goal for 15 attending guests** with a small thank you gift for the hostess for achieving the goal.
- **Providing your hostess with a save-the-date email** that she can forward to her friends in advance of receiving an invitation so they will reserve the date.
- **Mailing the invitations for your hostess.** Printed invitations will increase attendance since the guest has a tangible, visual reminder and will not be as likely to forget the date.
- **Making reminder calls for your hostess** to save her time and assure that guests remember the date and time. When the hostess calls her friends, they may get into a lengthy chat. When you make the calls to her friends, the conversations will be short and to the point. For any guest who cannot attend, offer your next available date for her to schedule her own show so she can enjoy a fun girls' night out with her friends and see the products in person.

2. At the Show

While traditional hostess coaching normally ends the minute the show begins, relationship building is just getting warmed up. Continue to intentionally and purposefully connect with your hostess with the following steps:

- **Connect with your hostess in a hostess huddle** just before the guests arrive to confirm her goals for the show and assure her that you are on the same page.
- **Invite her to put herself in your shoes** as she watches what you do throughout the show. It is like Cinderella. When she tried on the shoe, it fit. Your "shoes" just may fit for your hostess. "Sarah, watch what I do tonight and put yourself in my shoes. Then tell me what you think later."
- **Re-connect with her prior to leaving** to see what she liked best about "your shoes," and then invite her to talk further about the career opportunity. It is a gracious and non-pushy way to open the recruiting conversation with every hostess at every show. You might say to your hostess, "Sarah, how did the shoes fit? What would you think about doing what I do?"

3. After the Show

This is where you have the opportunity to make the most important strides in building relationships. Why? Because most hostesses are used to direct sellers who practice the "love 'em and leave 'em" syndrome. Here are the most important of all the hostess relationship-building steps:

- **Set her next show.** Before leaving her home that night, offer to tentatively schedule another show for her five to six months in advance, in a new season with new products. I call this the Dentist Principle, as that is what a dentist does every six months. You could say "Sarah, I know Tuesday is your favorite show night, so let's pencil you in for a Tuesday in March for our new season."
- **Send her a handwritten thank you** card the day after her show.
- **Submit her show orders within two days** and email her to confirm the delivery schedule. Your hostess and guests will appreciate your

urgency. Also, if you have overlooked anything and have guest or hostess questions, you can get them handled in a timely manner.

- **Send her an email listing the dates** of all the bookings from her show and letting her know you look forward to seeing her again.
- **Call her one month after her show** to confirm that she and her guests have received their products, and to share tips and answer questions. Ask her for referrals of those who did not attend so you can connect with them for future bookings.
- **Reconnect with her each month by phone just to check in** to see what she might need and how you can be of help. No need to worry about phone phobia when you connect with her each month because it is like checking in on a friend. This is the key to eliminating phone phobia!
- **Send her your monthly e-newsletters with tips,** ideas and new products, so that she hears from you monthly, thus continuing to build the relationship. Always encourage her referrals so you can continue to build your business daily with new leads.
- **Invite her to your hostess-only events during the year** such as special open house events, hostess teas and opportunity nights.
- **Send her a birthday card as well as greeting cards** for various holidays throughout the year.
- **Provide personal shopper service for her husband** or other family members when her birthday, anniversary or other gift occasion approaches where your product would be an appreciated gift. Your hostess will love you for it, and her husband will appreciate your help.

Customer Relationship Building

Even though your contact with your customers is usually not as frequent as with your hostesses, you still have an opportunity to connect and build a relationship in a purposeful, intentional way.

1. Before the Show

Break the ice and begin to build a relationship with customers using the following steps:

- **Jot a personal note on each guest's invitation** letting her know you look forward to meeting her.
- **Make reminder calls prior to the show to introduce yourself** and let them know you are looking forward to meeting them.

2. At the Show

Continue to build a relationship with customers using the following steps:

- **Meet each customer at the door and learn their names**—name tags are an easy, polite way to help with this process.
- **Engage in small talk,** such as what keeps her day busy, how she knows the hostess and how she knows your company.
- **Interact during the presentation** by having each customer share her favorite products, her needs related to your products, as well as upcoming gift occasions.
- **Share your career opportunity during the presentation** in a variety of non-pushy methods such as displaying signs in pretty picture frames saying, "Put yourself in my shoes—this job fits all sizes!", "Help wanted—more consultants needed in this area," "Control your schedule while earning a great paycheck—ask me how." Also, provide a play-money $1000 bill for each guest. Then ask them to write on the bill what they would do with an extra $1000 each month. Have them share their ideas. Explain this is what a consultant can earn with one or two average shows each week. Then ask the guest to write on the bill the name of someone they know who could use an extra $1000 each month. Invite each guest to share that information with you when you speak with her during ordering time. Finally, have a colorful, seasonally-themed display of recruiting brochures at your order taking area so you can easily refer to them, inviting each guest to take one home.

- **Have some personal consulting time with each guest** while she is placing her order. This is the number one most important time during every show as you have the opportunity to personally assist each guest and take steps toward building a relationship. Provide a place where you can sit one-on-one with each guest for a few minutes to confirm her order, suggest complementary products, invite her to pick a show date on your calendar and graciously offer career information. Say, "Let's pick a date to treat you and your friends to a fun girls' night out." In order to avoid a line of waiting guests from forming, create and place a sign next to a small tray that says, "Please place your order form here. I'll call you up next. Meanwhile, please enjoy some refreshments with our hostess and the other guests."

3. After the Show

Like with your hostess, the time after the show will provide the most important relationship-building opportunities with your customers. The following steps will help eliminate phone phobia and cure the "love 'em and leave 'em" syndrome. This is the three-step process that will make a huge difference in the success of your business and is what most direct sellers ignore:

- **Make a thank you phone call to each customer the day after the show** to let her know how much you enjoyed meeting her, thank her for being there and let her know you look forward to staying in touch.
- **Include each customer on your monthly e-newsletter distribution** so you stay in touch. This continues to foster your relationship with them and helps keep you on their mind.
- **Make customer courtesy calls monthly to check in with each customer** and see how you can be of assistance. Just like with your hostesses, if you stay in touch monthly just to check in, you need not worry about awkward phone phobia moments. Instead, you

will be connecting with a friend. Say something like, "Hi Jamie! I'm just checking in to see what you might need this month."

Examine the systems you currently have in place for hostess coaching and customer service. Then commit to becoming more intentional and purposeful about building relationships using the steps outlined in this chapter. You will find that you will increase your sales, bookings and recruiting, eliminate phone phobia and cure the "love 'em and leave 'em" syndrome. You will also create consistency in your business and reduce cancellations. Most importantly, you will build your business at the highest level of integrity and enjoy the many rewards relationship building can bring you.

BETH JONES-SCHALL
Spirit of Success, Inc.

Training that lifts you higher
—Isaiah 40:31

(303) 617-9968
beth@spiritofsuccess.com
www.spiritofsuccess.com

Beth is founder and president of Spirit of Success, Inc., a professional speaking and training company headquartered near Denver, Colorado. Beth's clients include Fortune 500 companies, government agencies, the military, schools, churches and numerous direct sales companies. Beth is listed in the International Who's Who of Entrepreneurs and has been honored with the YWCA Women of Achievement Award for her work.

She is a contributing author to the bestselling direct sales books, *Build It BIG* and *More Build It BIG*, as well as a member of the DSWA Board of Directors.

With over 25 years in the profession, Beth's direct sales experience has been extensive. As a top seller and recruiter, she has led over 1000 sales consultants producing sales of $10 million annually. She was also a corporate trainer for a leading direct sales company. Because Beth understands the unique needs of the direct selling profession, she is a sought-after speaker for conventions and leadership conferences. She brings humor along with practical, can-do skills to every presentation. Attendees rave at the immediate results they experience after applying the tools they've learned. Beth embodies the true meaning of the spirit of success!

Listen for Leads
Prospecting Made Fun and Easy

By Mary McLoughlin

In today's world you advance in life and business based on the quantity and quality of your networks, your connections and your relationships. Job opportunities, romantic relationships, friends and business partners begin with an introduction. Introductions happen in person, online, through social media, by request and by chance. It's what happens after the introduction that changes our lives.

We can approach our expanding networks in several ways. First, we can work to meet all kinds of people and let the relationships that form dictate how they fit into our lives; or we can select a purpose, such as leads for our business, and look for people who are a match. Either way involves meeting new people.

One way to find new people to meet is to expand our warm market. Have you created a list of prospects? If you are in sales, you probably have been asked to create a list of 100. If you have gone job hunting, you may have created a list of potential employers. If you are looking for a mate, you may have created a list of potential partners.

As a direct seller, you may wonder why the sales or parties that began with your friends and family did not work out as well as you had planned. One possibility is this: Your closest contacts will help you with your business because they want to help you. They may or may not have a vested interest or any interest in your products or services. When you venture a few degrees away from your closest connections, you will find people who are comfortable telling you "no, thank you." They also are much more likely to be invested in your product or service when they say yes, because they do not feel the obligation to help you. The results of these business connections may be more profitable.

Look and Attract

Finding leads begins with being intentional. It starts with creating a plan. Start by making a list of all the ways you know to find and attract leads. What has worked for you in the past? Are there ideas on your list that you have never tried? Who do you know that is successful in using these strategies? Where can you learn more about a particular strategy? Select one method at a time and become an expert. These strategies will help you start your list.

Create an Expanded Network Using a Mind Map

Finding leads begins with being intentional. Starting with a blank sheet of paper can be daunting. By creating a mind map and revisiting it regularly, you will find your lead base growing quickly. By learning to be intentional in attracting leads, you will find leads coming to you.

Let's create an expanded network that begins with you. Mind maps have been used for centuries to help with brainstorming, visual thinking and problem solving. On a blank sheet of paper, draw a circle in the center. Write your name in the circle. Draw rays from the circle, as in a sun. On each ray, write a name or place that represents the people from each part of your life. Examples include family, coworkers, spouse's coworkers, neighbors, church members, child's school friends, soccer team, high school friends, etc. Include categories that represent people from your present and people from your past. Attach branches to each ray with names of people from that group.

Here's an example of mind mapping: On my family branch, I have a son, Eric, who married my daughter-in-law, Laura. Her mom is Phyllis. Phyllis' best friend is Angela. Angela shares an office with Miles. Miles went to high school with my husband, and his wife, Ronna, is a friend I have not connected with in a few years. When I contacted Ronna, she held a show for me and led me to an entirely new group of people. If I had not drawn the map, I might not have remembered Ronna. Do you see how six degrees of separation really does lead back to you?

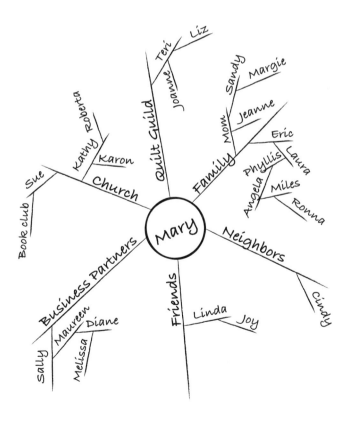

Spend some time drawing your map. Think into the past. Get out the high school yearbook, church directory, sports team roster, phone list from work and more. Post your map somewhere you can see it regularly. Who appears on your map? Did you discover people that don't yet know about your business? What would your reaction be if you discovered someone on the map had joined your company under someone else? Continue adding branches until you come to a dead end, then share your map. Show your map to a friend, family member or spouse. Ask them to add names to your map. Use it to make your list of prospects, and then set it aside. When you revisit it later, you will have met new people or remembered others. This is an ongoing, active map that will generate leads the entire time you are in business.

Become a Business Attractor

Another way to find leads is to become aware of what you are doing to attract people to your business. What would your best friend or your spouse say about your business? Because we are so comfortable around the people we know best, we easily drift into sharing our disappointments and the negative happenings in our businesses. Working with friends and family is a great privilege of direct selling. What are you doing to intentionally attract your family and friends to your business? Do you share stories of success? These can be much more than the financial success. Share stories of how you are growing as a person. Let them know what you are learning. Direct selling is unique in its opportunities for professional development. As you share your stories, others will come to learn of the great personal value in this industry as well as the financial possibilities.

Find ways to become a walking billboard. Wearing clothes and carrying totes with your company logo can stimulate conversations. If your company is well known, you will find people who are looking for you. If you represent a lesser-known company, you will attract questions. Be prepared with responses. As you connect with strangers, the goal is to invite them to learn more and to obtain their follow-up information. Be sure to have paper and pen handy at all times. Giving them your card or catalog and expecting them to call you will leave you staring at the phone. It's unlikely to ring.

Prepare a list of questions to ask when someone notices your logo. Here are a few to get you started:
- Do you own any of our products? What is your favorite?
- For party plan companies—have you ever attended or hosted a show?
- For network marketing companies—what kind of nutritional (or other appropriate category) products do you regularly use?

Remember, these will likely be quick conversations. You are listening for information that might lead to further interest. When you discover some, that's when you ask for their name and number to follow up. Then do make that follow-up call. For more information on the subject of follow-up, see Lyn-Dee Eldridge's chapter, *Follow-Up—How to Be Persistent and Respected*, that starts on page 167.

Listen to Learn

Direct selling is a relationship business. Quality relationships form as we get to know people. Learning to listen well can greatly increase your ability to quickly form strong relationships. You will also quickly learn how your products can serve others. For more on effective relationship building, read Beth Jones-Schall's chapter, *Build Your Business by Building Relationships* on page 111.

In order to understand the difference in quality listening, let's take a look at two different ways to listen. Think about the last time your best friend told you about something exciting that happened in her life. The conversation may have looked like this:

Carol: I just learned that I earned the trip to Jamaica with my company. I can't wait to go!

Ann: Wow, I love Negril, will you be going there?

Carol: I'm not sure. I don't have all the details.

Ann: You can't go to Jamaica without visiting Negril! It's the best part. Joe and I had an amazing time with the top salespeople in his team when we went. He was #2 in the company contest!

Carol: Good for him, I'm sure my trip won't be nearly as exciting as the one he won.

This is an example of Level One Listening, the kind we do with our head. Do you see what happens when you listen with your head? You are processing all you hear through your own agenda. Do you see how quickly the conversation focus turned from Carol to Ann? In this example Ann didn't let the conversation be about Carol's success, nor did Carol feel heard or celebrated. The conversation ended with Carol feeling disappointed, not excited, unlike when she shared her big news. Do you think Carol will be eager to share good news with Ann next time?

Watch what happens when the listening shifts to Level Two or heart-centered listening, as discussed in the DSWA trainings. This concept is discussed in the *Principle-Centered Coaching* program, as well as in the members-only teleclass, "Heart-Centered Listening™." Both are found on the DSWA website at www.dswa.org.

Carol: I just learned that I earned the trip to Jamaica with my company. I can't wait to go!

Ann: Congratulations! When is the trip?

Carol: Its November 5–10. I wonder what the weather is like then in Jamaica?

Ann: When we went in December, it was in the 80s. I'm sure it will be warm. Do you have your wardrobe ready?

Carol: Wow, I didn't even think about that. I need to go shopping quickly before all the summer clothes are out of the stores.

Ann: Want to plan a shopping date? I would love to help you find the perfect outfits and hear all the details.

Carol: That sounds perfect, I can't stop talking or thinking about this trip. I'm glad I have you to share my excitement with me.

Ann: I am so happy for you. This is quite an accomplishment.

Did you notice that when Ann stayed with Carol's excitement and story she learned more about Carol? She kept asking questions. Even when Ann added information about her own trip, she connected it to helping Carol plan her trip. Ann quickly learned that Carol could use some help shopping for the trip. The relationship continued as they planned for a shopping date. Carol felt heard and valued. She wanted to spend more time with Ann. Keeping the focus on Carol and asking questions are key skills of heart-centered listening™.

When we take time to find out about others and really listen, they want to be in relationship with us. We make them feel important. Let's look at how this kind of listening could make a difference as you look for leads. So often when we are prospecting, we are focused on what we will receive. It's all about sharing our business and asking for help. It's not uncommon to forget to slow down long enough to learn something about the other person. We wonder why we hear so little response. By taking time to listen to others, even the ones we are just meeting, they will feel important to us and heard. We can connect what we have to offer with what we learn about what they need. The following is a possible example of a conversation with someone from your mind map.

Joan: Hi, Angie. This is Joan. It's been awhile.

Angie: What a surprise to hear from you, it has been a long time.

Joan: Is this a good time to catch up?

Angie: Sure! Fill me in on the past few years.

Joan: I can't believe it's been that long. I recently started a new endeavor and began reconnecting with all of my friends and family. It's been great catching up with everyone. When I last saw you at the reunion, you had just moved to Ohio. How do you like living there?

Angie: You certainly have a good memory. My husband's job turned out great and after a bit of getting used to being away from family, we have adjusted nicely.

Joan: How do your children like their new school?

Angie: Once they got started in sports it has worked out great. It took a little time to make new friends. My daughter was in the eighth grade, and it was most difficult for her.

Joan: How about you, was it hard making new friends?

Angie: I knew I would have to step up and join a few things. Once I volunteered with the PTO and we found a good church, I made some great new friends. The Midwest is really a friendly part of the country. I tried working part-time, but with the kids' schedules and Dave's travel I decided it worked better to be at home.

Joan: Do you miss working?

Angie: I do miss having a few dollars of my own to spend. Did you say something about a new endeavor? Is that a new job?

Did you notice that Joan was up front about the reason she called? She shared a genuine interest in reconnecting with Angie, while letting her know that she had a reason to call. Joan confirmed that Angie had time and was interested in connecting. She kept the conversation focused on Angie until Angie asked about her reason for calling. If your reason to call is only to share your business, others will notice. Joan was open about how her new endeavor brought Angie to mind, but made it clear that it was a great opportunity to reconnect. The important message here is that you are genuine. If you really don't want to reconnect, don't fake it. Letting go of expectations is a key piece of heart-centered listening™. Whatever the results of the conversation, they are good results.

Observe and Serve

Putting your focus on the other person will guide you on how to best serve her with your business. In the example above, Joan learned that Angie missed having a few dollars of her own and that her family has a demanding schedule. Remember, even when you discover a need, it's important to share your business without expectation of the outcome. This conversation could continue in several different directions:

Joan: Actually, I just started my own direct selling business with XYZ company. I, too, needed something very flexible that would reward me well for my time. Have you ever checked out anything like this?

Angie: I did consider ABC company a few years back. I just wonder how it would fit into my life.

Joan: Would you be interested in hearing more about my company and how it might fit?

Angie: Sure, tell me more.

After sharing about the basics of her business, Joan might receive one of these responses:

Angie: That sounds great, how do I get started?

Or

Angie: No way would I have time for that.

Or

Angie: I am just not good at selling.

Joan: I know it's not for everyone. Tell me, can you think of one of your friends from church or PTO who might be interested?

Angie: My friend Anne might be.

Joan: Are you comfortable connecting us?

Joan might also ask Angie if she would be interested in her product. Leaving Angie feeling that any answer is okay with Joan will protect their relationship and leave Angie feeling that the phone call really was about her, not about Joan attempting to sell her on her company.

Using these approaches, your network will grow as others come to know you as a person who listens and is of service. As you learn to really listen to others, you will make wonderful connections. When people really feel heard, they feel valued. In fact, most often the feeling of being heard is connected to the feeling of being loved. You will soon become known as the business person who really does care about her customers. Your friends will be comfortable referring people to you. They will also be comfortable in their relationship with you, knowing that you respect their decision around your business, even if they are not interested. Imagine the joy your business will bring when you base it on serving others. The quality relationships you develop this way are certain to bring endless referrals.

MARY MCLOUGHLIN
Speaker, Trainer, DSWA Certified Coach

Helping build lives that matter

(614) 216-2055
mary@marymcloughlin.com
www.marymcloughlin.com

Mary began her direct selling career as a young mom looking for some extra income without compromising her commitment to raising her children. Over the next eighteen years, that little part-time business grew into a team that generated over $2 million in annual sales. In her role as a company leader, Mary was a featured speaker and trainer at national conferences and events.

Through her passion, training and coaching skills, Mary developed forty downline teams. She truly is a leader of leaders.

Mary's enthusiasm for the lifestyle created by blending work and family is contagious as she shares the stories, struggles and strategies that have created her success as well as the success of many others.

Mary is a certified DSWA ELITE Leader, one of the first graduates of the DSWA Coach Excellence School and is the Midwest Chapter Coordinator for the DSWA.

People Smarts
Building the Powerful Skills of Connection

By Cindy Sakai, MA, CDC

Do you ever get frustrated that some people are receptive to you while others cannot be bothered? Are you boggled by why some people take longer to make a buying decision than others? Do you want to understand why some of your consultants seem goal-oriented while others are not?

Understanding why people do the things they do is not an easy task. Sometimes it can make you want to pull your hair out. As a business professional in the direct sales industry, the more you understand what makes people tick, the greater your success. Your success starts with building strong connections with your current and potential customers; past, potential and current hostesses; current members of your team and any potential team members.

As you know, communicating, connecting and building rapport can be difficult and missteps can cost you business. In this chapter we are going to delve into a way to make all of your interactions much easier. The DISC behavioral style information provides a solid, methodical process to building rapport and relationships. You will learn how to make powerful people connections by:

- Understanding the behavioral style of others and their emotional needs
- Knowing how to deepen people's commitment by adapting to their communication style
- Learning strategies that make it easy for your prospects to take their next step

By understanding what makes people tick and what their emotional needs are, you will be able to provide them better service and support as you interact with them. Other people will feel understood and valued as you deliver the information that they truly need in a style that they most appreciate. This immediately creates stronger bonds, allowing for relationships to grow, and stronger relationships lead to more business and success for you.

The Impact of Behavior Styles on Connections

"Seek first to understand before being understood."
—Stephen Covey, speaker, author

You can have the best opportunity presentation, the best products and the best speaking skills, but if your information and value don't translate to your prospect's needs, the "greatness" of what you offer is useless. Your effectiveness and success in any new connection starts with knowing the emotional needs of the other person and then knowing how to meet them.

An easy and laser-like way to understand what makes people tick is to learn about four basic behavioral styles called DISC. DISC teaches us how to slice through the complexity of people's behaviors and puts them into the four easy-to-remember styles of Dominance, Influence, Steadiness and Conscientiousness.

You will find that you can use DISC to impact relationships in all realms of your life. There are three steps to using DISC effectively:
- Self-Awareness: Know your natural behavioral style
- People-Reading: Identify your prospect's DISC style
- Adapting: Connect with your prospect by adapting to their DISC style

I will help you understand the tendencies of each DISC style and provide you strategies for relating to your prospect in a way that they feel most appreciated.

Guidelines to Remember When Using DISC

1. There is no right or wrong style. Each style has its own strengths as well as weaknesses. When working with a team, the diversity of styles makes a stronger team.

2. You have all four styles of DISC. One or two styles may be naturally stronger for you than the others, but you have all four styles in you. DISC is not a tool to stereotype people.

3. You tend to use the style that will enable you to be successful in a situation. For example, if your strongest style is Influence, during an emergency, your natural tendency to chit-chat would subside, and you would probably see the Dominance style emerge.

Step #1: Self-Awareness

It is critical to have a strong sense of your own personal selling style if you are going to be effective at enrolling others. You need to know what motivates you, how you define success and your natural strengths. One reason to know this is to clearly understand what qualities have made you successful to this point. It is also important to know your strengths because when they are over-exercised or used too often, your strengths can become your weaknesses. You will begin to overvalue your personal preferences and forget to create an environment where all styles feel welcome, motivated and can achieve success.

The best way to learn about your style is to complete one of Inscape Publishing, Inc's DiSC® Profiles (Everything DiSC® for Sales, Everything DiSC® for the Workplace or Everything DiSC® for Management) at www.think-training.com. In the meantime, a quick, less comprehensive way to assess your style is to use the grid below. In the following columns, check off the five words that describe you best:

Column #1	Column #2	Column #3	Column #4
☐ Bold	☐ Optimistic	☐ Cooperative	☐ Accurate
☐ Goal-oriented	☐ Sociable	☐ Patient	☐ High standards
☐ Tell it like it is	☐ Enjoy being with people	☐ Good listener	☐ Private
☐ Decisive	☐ Lack follow-through	☐ Have a difficult time saying no	☐ Analytical
☐ Adventuresome	☐ Trusting	☐ Stable	☐ Analysis paralysis

The column with the most checks will reveal your preferred DISC style:

Column #1—Dominance Style. You believe that success comes from setting and pursuing goals. You are not afraid to talk to anyone about your opportunity. If someone says no to you, you move onto the next and never think twice about it.

Column #2—Influence Style. You believe that success will come through knowing people personally and professionally. You spend time building friendships. If someone says no to you, you may take it personally and wonder what you did wrong.

Column #3—Steadiness Style. You believe that success will come when you have a solid plan to take care of the business process and people in it. You do not take on challenges without thinking it through to ensure that it is safe and sensible. You probably hold off on asking people to commit because you do not want to pressure people to make decisions.

Column #4—Conscientiousness Style. You believe that success will come when you know everything about the business. You are accurate, organized and thorough. You may have a tendency to be overly thorough and miss the opportunity to enroll a team member.

Step #2: People-Reading

Building powerful people connections requires you to identify your prospect's DiSC style. We call this "people-reading." When people-reading, ask yourself two key questions about your prospect's behaviors. The two answers combined help you determine a person's DISC style.

Question #1: Is this person fast-paced and outgoing or slow-paced and reserved?

Question #2: Is this person more matter-of-fact or people-oriented?

	Matter-of-fact	or	**People-oriented**
Fast-paced & outgoing	DOMINANCE		INFLUENCE
Slow-paced & reserved	CONSCIENTIOUSNESS		STEADINESS

In the following sample encounter with the Influence Style, the underlined phrases are people-reading clues to help determine the DISC style.

When I met Jane for the first time, she was a <u>burst of energy</u>. The first thing I noticed was her <u>big smile</u> as she was <u>talking with another person</u>. When she turned to greet me, she introduced herself, "Hi, welcome, I'm so glad you were able to make it tonight. I'm Jane. What's your name?" I introduced myself as she <u>looked me straight in the eyes and smiled</u>. We <u>chatted</u> for just a bit as she <u>asked about my son</u> who was with me. I left <u>feeling energized</u> by her <u>bubbly energy</u>.

From this brief encounter, Jane's outgoing and people-oriented behavior shows us that her style for the moment is Influence.

Step #3: Engage by Adapting to Your Prospect's DISC Style

Once you have identified your prospect's DISC style, it's time to adapt to it and meet her emotional needs. Chances are you tend to lead your interactions based on your natural style. But, what if the behaviors typical of your own natural DISC style clash with the needs of your prospect? The key is to adapt your style for the moment. For example, if your style is naturally Conscientiousness and your prospect has the Dominance style, you would need to fight the urge to provide too many details and you would need to adapt by presenting the opportunity at a quick rate of speech, in a top three-bullet-point format, connecting the opportunity directly to her goals. Lastly, you would want to ask her to commit that day, offering two different options. The D Style loves options and wants to feel in control of her outcomes.

Here is an example of a conversation with the Dominance style:
"Thank you for coming to tonight's presentation, I am <u>certain</u> that this is the perfect opportunity for you. Our <u>business model</u> has the potential to help you reach your declared financial goal within six months. This is a great opportunity to be a <u>pioneer</u> with this product for your area. It is a <u>risk worth taking</u> because <u>you control your rewards</u>. What you put in is exactly what you get out. <u>The sky is the limit</u>. Would you like to get started with plan A or plan B?"

In this conversation, the underlined words appeal to the Dominance style's eagerness to drive results, confidence and willingness to take risks in an adventure. As you interact with each person, you have the opportunity to make the most of that moment, hook their attention and motivate them to a next step. This is true for each prospect, hostess or team member you have in front of you.

Here are some success strategies for working with each DISC Style:

Engaging the Dominance Style
The Dominance style is fast and no-nonsense. When engaging with this style, you have a short time window to hook their attention and get to the next action step. Remember the following when connecting with the Dominance style:

"D" Mottos
"Just Do It"
"Results = Success"

Characteristics of the Dominance style
- Uses a fast-paced approach
- Focuses on the bottom line and getting results
- Can be impatient
- Likes to be in control in order to drive results
- Is excited by adventure and challenges
- Success philosophy: We will be successful if we relentlessly pursue solid goals
- Strength: Decisive risk-taker
- Weakness: Working with people
- They ask confirming questions: "Will it do this for me?" "Can I earn XX income?"
- Decisions tend to be quick

How to communicate to the Dominance style
- Be direct and get straight to the point
- Communicate bottom-line results up front to maintain their attention
- Do not sugarcoat information or beat around the bush
- Demonstrate confidence and competence
- Hook their attention with words such as achieve, control, succeed, accomplish and results

What motivates the Dominance style into action
- Be clear about rules and expectations
- Clarify goals—the Dominance style is very goal-oriented
- Let them initiate action
- Give them freedom and autonomy

• Publicly recognize their ability to set and achieve goals

Engaging the Influence Style

The social and networking nature of the direct sales industry naturally attracts the Influence style. When engaging with this style, taking time to create a personal connection is important. Remember the following when connecting with the Influence style:

"I" Mottos
"I love people!"
"Let's do lunch"

Characteristics of the Influence style
• Fast-paced
• Talkative and sociable
• Casual, relaxed and unstructured
• Success philosophy: We will be successful if everyone is having fun and enjoying each other
• Strength: Fosters strong relationships
• Weakness: Time management and organization
• They ask a lot of personal questions: "What would you do if you were me?"
• Decisions tend to be quick

How to communicate to the Influence style
• Use a fast-paced approach
• Be energetic and enthusiastic
• Communicate informally with touches of humor
• Let them know about testimonials and who is using your product or services
• Engage them with phrases such as *influence and help others, exciting opportunity* and *you'll love…*, etc.

What motivates the Influence style into action

- Help them see how your product/service will increase their ability to influence and help others
- Provide continuous feedback
- Create a team/group atmosphere
- Stay in touch and connect often

Engaging the Steadiness Style

This style appears cool, calm and collected. The style strives to create a stable and steady environment and thrives when they can plan for what is to come. Big changes rock their boat. However, you get their buy-in when they can see a plan for implementation. Remember the following when connecting with the Steadiness style:

"S" Mottos
"All for one, one for all."
"Don't make waves."

Characteristics of the Steadiness style

- Uses a slow-paced approach
- Tends to be reserved
- Focuses on keeping a stable environment
- Organized and structured
- Loyal, tactful, nurturing
- Success philosophy: We will be successful if we have a good plan and a team of people who work harmoniously together
- Strength: Great at getting people to feel comfortable and cared for
- Weakness: Has a difficult time asking for the sale
- They ask lots of "how" questions: "How do I handle it when someone wants to return a product?" "How do you know that this is a better product?"
- Decisions tend to be slow

How to Communicate to the Steadiness style
- Use a slow-paced approach
- Present information in an organized way
- Point out safeguards for your product/services such as warranties and money-back guarantees
- Use words such as *plan, structure, safeguards, predict* and *thank you*

What motivates the Steadiness style into action
- Words of appreciation
- A clear plan of next steps
- Clear expectations

Engaging the Conscientiousness Style

This style values quality, excellence and accuracy. It's all about the details! Details help build their confidence in your products and services. You will want statistics, graphs and brochures with you when presenting to a C style. Remember the following when connecting with the Conscientiousness style:

"C" Mottos
"Just the facts, please."
"More details, please"

Characteristics of the Conscientiousness style
- Uses a slow-paced approach
- Tends to be reserved
- Focuses on accuracy, quality and excellence
- Appreciates a logical approach
- Extremely detail-oriented
- Success philosophy: We will be successful if we make accurate decisions and are meticulous about everything we do
- Strength: Accuracy, tracking and follow-through

- Weakness: Difficult time asking for the sale
- They ask lots of "why" questions: "Why do we do it that way?" "Why is it better than the competitor's?"
- Decisions tend to be slow

How to communicate to the Conscientiousness style:
- Use a slow-paced approach
- Provide details
- Allow extra time for questions
- Have brochures or information available to provide more details
- Use words such as accuracy, quality, excellence, research and statistics

What motivates the Conscientiousness style into action:
- A logical next step
- Information and details to make a well-thought-out decision
- Knowing that your product/services will add quality and excellence to their life

What's Next? Practice, Practice, Practice!

As with any new skill, it simply takes practice to make DISC a part of how you build powerful connections with your business partners. Here are some recommendations to help you increase your "people smarts" using DISC:

1. Practice people-reading every day and you will see the different styles emerge. Most importantly, practice adapting to the four styles.

2. Use DISC language to take your people skills to the next level. Look and recognize the value that each person brings to the team, and avoid judging people who are different from you.

3. Deepen your knowledge about DISC and become masterful at applying it to impact recruiting, sales, team effectiveness and personal effectiveness. Consider taking an Inscape Publishing, Inc. research-based DiSC® profile assessment to understand your natural strengths and weaknesses. Go to www.think-training.com for DiSC®

related resources for individual effectiveness, team effectiveness, management skills, and sales skills.

Understanding the behavioral needs of yourself and others will make you more effective at selling and enrolling new prospects. When you build relationships by focusing on self-awareness, people-reading and adapting, you will find that your relationships become more comfortable and effective. The little things that frustrated you about people melt away, connections deepen, and new opportunities show up. People feel good about being with you; they feel understood. And in the process of meeting and making new connections, you will have more fun with every person you meet.

CINDY SAKAI, MA, CDC
TH!NK, LLC

Helping leaders dream big and produce results

(808) 936-4992
cindy@think-training.com
www.think-training.com

As a Training Resultant and Certified Dream Coach®, Cindy Sakai believes that anything is possible if you believe in yourself. She inspires people to dream big and gain clarity on how to make it happen. As the co-owner of a training and development company, TH!NK, LLC, Cindy inspires and teaches leaders how to create their dream workplaces where team members love coming to work and thrive during times of change. TH!NK, LLC's high-content programs help people build trust, have powerful one-on-one conversations, and build stronger teams.

Since 2000, TH!NK, LLC has worked with organizations such as the U.S. Army, Oceanic Time Warner Cable, McDonalds Restaurants of Hawaii, YMCA and Goodwill Industries of Hawaii, to name a few. With experience in the direct sales industry and as an officer of the Direct Selling Women's Alliance Sonoma-Marin Chapter, Cindy teaches direct sales professionals how to build trust and loyalty with their customers and business partners.

Cindy holds an MA in Organizational Management and is certified in the Leadership Development Process™, the DISC system of behavioral styles, the Dream Coach Process® and as a Trained Purposeful Coach.

146

The Art of Persuasive Selling
How to Influence Prospects
with Suggestive Booking Bids

By Tammy Stanley

Imagine just for a moment that you are in a workshop setting and I ask you to come to the front of the room. I ask you to stand next to me and face the audience while you place the palm of your left hand against the palm of my right hand. Then rather unexpectedly, I begin to push rather forcefully against the palm of your hand. What do you think you would do?

If you answered that you would push back, you are like all the volunteers who ever come up to the front of the room at one of my workshops. This exercise demonstrates that prospects naturally resist. Resisting is not only how prospects protect their pocketbook, but it is also how they show that they have a mind of their own and can think for themselves.

Think About What Your Prospects Are Thinking

Now think about the last time you went to a home product party. Is it possible that on the drive over to the hostess' home you had a good talk with yourself that went something like this: "Whatever happens tonight, under no circumstances am I going to book a party." If that has ever happened to you, you started resisting the idea of booking a party even before you arrived at the hostess' home and met the direct seller conducting the party.

Direct sellers are often surprised when they have difficulty getting the guests at their home parties to book a party. The key is to remember what it is like to be one of those guests. When you remember what it is like to be a guest, you begin to realize that a guest attending a home party is not much different than you—for whatever reasons she might have decided on the drive over that she is not going to book a party.

Now before you decide that I am just a "Negative Nelly," understand that by looking at the way things really are you have tremendous power to change the things that need improving. One of the most beneficial ways to improve the number of bookings that you generate at each home party is to better understand your prospects so that you address their concerns and needs. The best way to gain any prospect's interest is to tap into the conversation that is already going on in the prospect's mind.

Certainly it is wonderful if you have found a particular company's product line so beneficial that you decided to start selling it. However, the guests attending your home parties are not going to suddenly be receptive to booking a party just because you have decided to sell, no matter how much better you think the product line is compared to that of another company. You generate far more bookings at each and every home party when you dare to look at the conversation that is already going on in the minds of the guests who attend those parties.

Daring to consider that the guests arriving at a home party have no intention of booking a party can actually be good for your business, as long as you prepare to persuade them otherwise! Certainly seeing the product line in person and having fun with friends can begin to wear down the resistance of a guest. By the end of the night a guest who had no intention of booking a party might agree to book a party after all. It is very important to realize that many guests want to wait until the following season to book their parties.

Upgrade Your Booking Bid

The only way to ensure that you secure those coveted bookings in your calendar now—as opposed to later—is to look at the conversation going on in the minds of your guests and to influence the conclusions and decisions they will make. The easiest way to persuade a guest to want to book a party of her own is by making statements that handle her concerns and objections.

Most direct sellers are familiar with the idea of making a booking bid. The majority of direct sellers probably employ a booking bid similar to the following:

"There are several ways to get these products. One way is by purchasing them as a guest tonight. But another way is by being a hostess and getting what you want for free."

Yes, that is a booking bid, but does it motivate your guests to book now instead of later? Probably not. The reason why that booking bid does little to convince someone to book a party now is because it simply restates something that the vast majority of guests at a home party already know. Most guests at a home party are not thinking, *"I definitely would book a party if I found out that I could earn free products by doing so."* The guests already know that they can earn free products by booking a party, and restating what they already know is not how you increase their desire to book a party with you *today*.

A good demonstration certainly can inspire a guest to have a wish list bigger than her pocketbook, and that can persuade a guest to host a party and get some of the products for free. However, to dramatically increase bookings, you want to consider more reasons to book a party than just earning free products. In addition to that, you want to look at the obstacles that typically get in the way of a prospect booking a home party.

Some of the obstacles that often get in the way of a guest booking a party right away could be:
- Her current commitments with work and family keep her really busy
- She attempted to host a home party in the past but ended up getting very few guests to attend
- She does not feel she knows enough people to invite to make the party successful
- Her home seems too small for entertaining

Some of the reasons a guest may desire to book a home party could be to:
- Introduce her friends to a great product line
- Provide a night of entertainment and fun for her friends
- "Test the waters" by seeing how her friends react to a product line she is secretly thinking about selling herself
- Get to know you better
- Help you in your business

When you have booking bids that touch upon those reasons and obstacles for booking a home party, you increase your chances of tapping into the conversation already going on in the mind of a guest. Your words speak to the subconscious mind, which incorporates the ideas you present as part of the inner dialog of your prospect. You persuade your prospect to book a party without her even noticing you doing so. In other words, you persuade without resistance.

Understanding the Process of Persuasion

If you want to experience a sudden increase in bookings, it is important to understand how to persuade your prospects to accept the idea of hosting a party. Before anyone accepts an idea, they mentally move through the following six steps:

1. Total rejection
2. Partial rejection
3. Partial acceptance
4. Total acceptance
5. Partial assimilation
6. Total assimilation

Interestingly enough, the first step to accepting an idea is total rejection. Most guests arrive at a home party already convinced that they are not going to book a party themselves. When you first mention booking a party, those guests are in total rejection. By sprinkling numerous booking bids throughout your demonstration, you help to move your prospects through those six steps and you also increase the number of bookings you generate.

Let me give an example of a booking bid I might use to address the obstacle of feeling overwhelmed by one's busy schedule:

"I want to thank all of you for coming tonight. We all seem so busy these days, and I think one of the most positive things about a home party like this is that it gives us a chance to build a sense of community with our friends, family and acquaintances. When we feel a part of a community, we feel good about ourselves and we increase our capacity to get through some of life's challenges."

That probably sounded more like a philosopher speaking than a salesperson giving a booking bid, which is exactly why your prospects are likely to feel no resistance. When you make statements that fit in nicely with your prospects' own thinking, your prospects readily accept your ideas as their own. People do not argue with their own ideas, and consequently any guest who walked into this home product party thinking that she was too busy to host a show herself now might be thinking, "Wait a minute, it has been a long time since I have spent time with my friends, and it is important to stay connected with people, especially during tough times."

Knowing that many of your prospects refrain from booking because they feel too busy, you want to have more than one bid that handles that obstacle. After all, that first booking bid might move some people from "total rejection" to "partial acceptance," but it probably will not move them all the way to "total acceptance."

Speak to What Matters to Your Potential Hostesses

Keep in mind that anyone who considers hosting a home party wants to have a successful event. When a customer tells you that she does not have enough time to book a party, what she really means is that she does not have enough time to host a successful home party. In order to move your prospects further along the road to accepting the idea of booking a party, a few moments later you could say something like this:

"I like all my hostesses to save time and money. That is why I suggest exactly what our hostess tonight has done—a bowl of pretzels and a bowl of chocolate candies alongside a favorite beverage. Hosting a party really can be simple because your friends care most about getting together."

One aspect of a powerful booking bid is that it encourages your prospects to agree with you. When prospects are in a state of agreement with you, resistance is at an all-time low. By saying, "Your friends care most about getting together," you substantiate the concept of friendship, and any guest there who values her friends cannot resist agreeing with you.

By now I hope you can see how important it is to move your guests and your prospects along these steps of accepting the idea of hosting. When you sprinkle those types of booking bids throughout your home party demonstration, you find that your guests have far less resistance to booking a show. By sprinkling numerous bids that handle your prospects' most common obstacles, oftentimes the guests ask to book a party even before you have a chance to ask them.

Take a Few Cues From a Good Waiter

Imagine for a moment that you are at a fancy restaurant enjoying a meal with a few of your friends. The food is so delicious you eat everything on your plate, and considering American portions these days, you feel more than full. After clearing your dinner plates, your waiter, who is new on the job, asks if you saved room for dessert. You have no problem telling him that you did not.

Do you see how effortless it was to pass on dessert? More importantly, grasp how the waiter made it so easy for you to say no. This inexperienced waiter never even thought about maximizing the sale at your dinner table. Considering that servers earn most of their income by collecting 15 to 20 percent of the tab as a tip, they would profit far more by adopting the mind of a salesperson. The key to maximizing this selling situation would be for the waiter to recognize that the majority of his customers eat way too much of their entrée to ever consider ordering dessert. Once he acknowledges that simple fact, he can prepare to respond more deliberately.

When the waiter places your entrée on the table, he could say, "Enjoy your meal, but you might want to save some room for dessert. The chocolate pots here are truly sublime." Even if you do not care for chocolate pots, his suggestion could launch your brain into wondering what else the restaurant has on the dessert menu. In addition to that, you may decide to eat only half of the serving and to pack up the rest to take home. Amazing what one appropriately-timed suggestion can do, is it not?

Now imagine that instead of asking you whether or not you saved room for dessert, this waiter brings a dessert tray. Instead of simply pointing to each dessert, he describes each of them with vigor. By the time he is done, you yearn to taste not one, but several. Fortunately you have a few friends at the table, and you all decide on several desserts to share.

The only difference between these two scenarios is that the first waiter concentrated only on serving while the second waiter realized that the majority of his customers do not want dessert after eating a big meal. He came prepared to overcome that common obstacle.

Right now the only difference between you and the direct seller with a fully booked calendar is heightened preparation. Make a list right now of the three most common objections you hear about booking a party. After you have done that, develop a booking bid that handles each of those objections in a harmonizing manner. Practice delivering those booking bids, as you would practice a role in a play so that you do not feel nervous once you are at your next home party.

When you implement booking bids that speak more to the subconscious mind than the conscious mind, your prospects show less resistance because the ideas you communicate sound more like their own ideas than those of a salesperson trying to sell them something. The key is to begin with the conversation that might already be going through the minds of your prospects. When you concern yourself with what your prospects are thinking and feeling, you are guaranteed a higher conversion rate of guests who book a home party of their own.

TAMMY STANLEY
The Sales Refinery

A better bottom line is no laughing matter

(480) 775-4866
tammy@tammystanley.com
www.tammystanley.com

Tammy Stanley directs The Sales Refinery, a sales training firm that assists direct sellers in generating more business through powerful marketing, selling and leadership strategies. Known for her captivating storytelling, she analyzes and presents the often overlooked fundamental aspects of the selling process.

Tammy has been coaching and training since 1994 and has a deep understanding of the challenges and needs of the direct sales professional. While raising four children and using word-of-mouth advertising as her only mode of marketing, Tammy built a multi-million-dollar direct sales organization, reaching her company's Circle of Excellence seven years in a row. Her efforts earned numerous sales and leadership awards along with world travel, placing her in the top echelons of her field.

As a former senior executive in direct sales, Tammy believes sales people need more than motivation; they need the necessary tools to stop their own unproductive behaviors. Through her free weekly ezine, keynote presentations, workshops, books and audio CDs, she inspires audiences to develop the habits that yield success.

Tammy is passionate about dirct sales and the psychology behind sales. She is the author of the book, *Carpe Phonum: How to Seize the Phone Even When You Lack Courage*, published by TS Stanley, LLC in 2006.

Maximize Your Party

By Ruth Fuersten

From the moment you enter your hostess' home to do a show or party, until you leave, everything you say and do needs to be said and done with the idea of booking, selling and recruiting at the heart of it. Everything! Here are some little tweaks you can implement right away to increase your sales and bookings, plus create more interest in recruiting.

Before the Guests Arrive

During your set-up, bring up the idea of recruiting with your hostess. Simply say, "Sally, let's take a look at the orders you have." As you flip through them say, "Wow! You really did great. How did you like selling with (your company's name) for the past couple of weeks? Have you ever considered becoming a (your company's name) consultant?"

Her response, in all probability, is going to be no. Be ready for the "no" by finding out why she is reluctant to join you. "Really? I think you'd be great. What's stopping you from being a consultant?"

The usual responses are:
- Not enough time
- I don't like selling things
- I don't like to talk in front of people

Have a response for each of these objections. Remember, you are just chatting with your hostess. You are offering her the opportunity to tell you why, in a million years, she would not do what you are doing.

People do not always enroll the first time you bring it up to them. Knowing that, what can you say to create more interest in recruiting? Once you know what her reason is for saying no you could add, "I really do think you would be good doing this. Would you do me a favor and watch me tonight? Watch me critically, to see how hard I don't work." Then change the subject. Remember, you are just chatting with her. Just bring up the idea that you think she would be good doing what you are doing.

During the Show or Party

Increase your sales and bookings with your guest introductions. When you have the guests introduce themselves, have them tell you their favorite "fantastic" product and why they love it. Every person who purchased your products in the past is now providing you with a testimonial. There might be someone there who has never been to a party before, so she does not have a favorite product. When you get to her, just welcome her. By doing this one simple tweak, getting testimonials from the guests, you will increase the guests' interest in purchasing what their friends have and are raving about.

Find out if any former hostesses are on the guest list and come prepared with their show information. When you get to someone who has been a hostess for you in the past say, "Mary is a very special person to me because Mary is one of my beautiful, fabulous and wonderful hostesses. Mary, do you remember what you received just by having a show?" Having her information allows you to show everyone what she received as a hostess. Then give the statistics of her show. "Mary had ten buying guests and two bookings. Because of that she received $290 worth of products for only $75, including twenty of her favorite items. Mary, was it worth your time and effort to have a party?" All eyes are on her and she is going to say, "Yes, it was really fun!"

What you have done is taken the idea of booking out of the hypothetical and placed it firmly in reality. Instead of saying, "If you are a hostess this is what you might get," you are saying, "Look at everything this hostess received. Don't you want to get all of this, too?" This allows the guests to realize the benefits of booking right from the beginning of your presentation. You still have not started your presentation and already you have covered booking, selling and recruiting!

Start your product presentation with your highest-priced item to increase sales and bookings. So often we skip showing our most expensive item because we think people will not buy it due to the price. Your company provides you with those items as booking tools. Pass it around and talk about it. Come up with a reason why they have got to book a party so they can get it for less under your hostess program.

Think about your own behaviors when you are invited to a selling party. You have a pretty good idea of how much you are going to spend before you even get into the house. So do your guests. They watch your presentation, make their choices and wait for dessert. When you show your highest-priced item last they are going to look at it, think it is very nice, but they are not going to add it to their order. When you show it first, they fall in love with it and spend the rest of their time figuring out if they are going to buy it or book a show to get it.

Get higher sales with add-on sales by showing your lowest-priced items last. People will add on a lower-priced item if you give them a reason to do so.

159

Encourage guests to do what you are doing by telling your story.
When you talk about why you joined your company you need to take
into consideration why people decide to be recruited and join your
team. The two main reasons are: more time and money. Capitalize on
that. What is the minimum wage in your area? By knowing what you
make on average at your shows, you can figure out how many hours
someone needs to work at minimum wage to make what you make
doing one show a week.

*"I was looking for an additional stream of income so I started looking
into part-time jobs. What I discovered was they wanted me to be there
at least twenty hours a week and paid only minimum wage. I really
did not want to be gone from my family that long for so little pay.
When I looked into (your company) I discovered I could be gone for
only one night a week and make as much money as I would working a
minimum-wage job for twenty hours a week. So if you are like me and
you are looking for an additional stream of income, just let me know
and we will talk later."*

Use the door prize slip for maximum results. The more information
you have about people the more business you can do with them. Take
the time to have the guests fill out the door prize slip and go through
it with them for maximum results. A good door prize slip has at least
three questions on it:

Question One: Are you interested in being a (your company) hostess?
- Let them know what additional services you provide. Can you help
  her expand her wardrobe and have many more outfits with only a
  few pieces from the clothing company you represent? Can you help
  her with picture groupings for her walls with only a few items from
  the wall décor company you represent? Can you show her how to
  affordably make a week's worth of meals for her family with the

food product company you represent? Ask yourself what additional service you can provide a hostess because you are in her home.

• Tell the guests that if they are interested in having a party to mark "yes," and if they have questions about having a party to mark "maybe." Do not mention no. They are very good at finding that one all on their own. Providing them the opportunity to ask you questions privately will increase your bookings. They may never have been a hostess and don't know what to do or what is required. They may want to have a party with a friend and wonder if they can do that. These are "maybes" you can easily turn into "yeses."

Question Two: Are you interested in the (your company) opportunity?

• You can continue your story with the following: "Now I don't know about you, but I like to make a decision with information. If you are like I was and looking for an additional stream of income, go ahead and mark 'maybe.'" Do not tell them to mark "yes" because yes sounds like a commitment. They are not ready to make a commitment. Telling them to mark "maybe" sounds like, "I just want you to have the information you need to be able to make a decision."

• Go on to say, "I'll give you information tonight. You can take it home, read it and write down all your questions. In a couple of days I will call you and we will go over your questions. At the end of that call you will be giving me one of three responses:

• "You might say, 'Thanks for your time but this is not for me.' That is okay with me because you have come to that decision based on information. You might say, 'This is interesting. I would like a little more time to think about it.' That is a great response too. I will give you a few more days to write down all of your additional questions, and we will talk again.

• Or you might say, 'This is great. Where do I sign?' No matter which answer you give me, you have come to that decision with information and having gotten all of your questions answered."

Question Three: Are there any products you would be interested in if they go on special?

- Make sure your door prize slip says "special" and not "sale." Again, read them the question and say, "If there is anything you saw tonight that you would like to own in the future, go ahead and write it down. If it ever goes on special, I'll give you a call and let you know. Make sure you have your phone number on the top of your slip."

- At the end of the drawing put the door prize slips away. As you are taking orders you will be able to say, "I don't have the door prize slips in front of me and I can't remember, are you interested in having your own (your company name) party to take advantage of our hostess program, or are you interested in more information about the fantastic opportunity with (your company name)?" This allows you to be able to ask every guest if they want to book a show or sign up with your company.

After Another Successful Event

The guests have gone home and you are alone with your hostess. Start talking to her about recruiting again. "Sally, I think all of your friends had a good time tonight. Did you notice how hard I didn't work? You know, I still think you would make a great consultant. Now, before you turn me down I want to share a little bit of information with you about your party. First off, you had this amount in sales. That means that tonight, in your living room, I made this much money. Additionally, you received this many bookings, and if you become a consultant those would be your parties to help you get started. Not only that, but this many of your friends took home information about becoming a consultant. I would love to have you come into the company as my personal recruit and then we can put your friends under you as your personal recruits." Then tell her what it would mean to have that many people under her. "Just think of the fun you and your friends would have training together, making money together, going to our national conference and even earning vacations and trips. You could actually walk the beaches of the world with your friends. What questions do you have about becoming a consultant?"

She is going to say one of two things. She is either going to tell you "no" or she is going to start asking questions. In your excitement you might tend to stay and answer all of her questions. But at the end, what do most of them say? "I want to think about it." You leave and what does your hostess do? She straightens up the house and gets ready for the next day. Too many questions and post-party conversation gets her to bed too late. We want to avoid your now potential recruit from being so tired the next morning that she decides not to join you in the business.

To avoid this, as she starts to ask questions stay with her and answer a couple of them and then start packing. You can still answer questions as you pack up. Pack everything except your calendar and a recruiting package. Then say, "You know Sally, I could sit here all night and tell you the benefits I've received by being involved with (your company name), but you probably wouldn't be very happy with me if I did that. So how about if we do this: Here is a packet of information about the company. Go through this and write down all your questions. Then we can get together in a few days, close your show and I will answer all your questions." Get a date and get out the door. Leave her wanting more.

When you talk to your hostess or a guest about recruiting you want to hit on her hot button. Ask her, "I'm curious, why are you interested in the (your company name) opportunity?" Now you know why she took your information, and you can frame your responses around why she wants to join.

Keep your door prize slips for more sales. As your company comes out with booking specials or as you create your own specials, you can use the door prize slips to match the specials with the very people who told you they wanted those products. When you call them you can say, "Hi Pam, this is (your name) from (your company name). We met at Sally's when she had her party. Do you have a minute? You wrote on your door prize slip that you would be interested in this product if it ever went on special. I don't know if you would be interested, but it is a hostess special this month, and I just wanted to let you know that by having a party you can get that item for (explain your special). Is that something you would be interested in?"

She may book to get the item she wants. She may tell you she does not do parties. If that is the case then mark her slip as a sale only person. When the day comes and you need more sales to earn a trip or meet a goal you can pull out the "sale only" slips, call them, and offer them the products they want at a reduced price. Using the information they have provided you on the door prize slips is a way of working smarter—not harder.

To maximize your parties, always analyze what you have done to increase sales, bookings and recruits. Figuring out what you are doing that is working and what you are doing that has less than favorable results will reap long-term results. Be willing to try different things, new ideas and the suggestions you read here to get better and better at booking, selling and recruiting your way to greater and greater success.

RUTH FUERSTEN
America's Direct Sales Teacher

(715) 298-1656
ruth@booksellrecruit.com
www.booksellrecruit.com

A love of helping others inspires Ruth to assist direct sales women from around the world to advance their businesses and achieve their dreams. Her clients include a range of women, from those just starting out in direct selling to senior executive directors and company founders. Ruth's one-on-one and group coaching sessions are noted for being packed with information that is not only achievable, but can be immediately implemented.

The author of *How To Book, Sell and Recruit Your Way To Success*, Ruth works with regional leaders and companies to present teleseminars, workshops and live, in-person seminars that empower participants to dramatically increase their sales, bookings and recruiting leads. Emphasizing that everything you do at your presentation needs to be done to promote more bookings, higher sales and more leads, Ruth provides step-by-step directions and the wording to use.

Twenty-five years as a professional educator and over twelve years in direct sales gives Ruth the unique ability to teach consultants how to book, sell and recruit their way to success.

Follow-Up—How to Be Persistent and Respected

Building New Relationships and Creating a Warm Market

By Lyn-Dee Eldridge, CPC, CPMC

When you are passionate about your product, people feel your enthusiasm; they respond to your sincerity and the magic begins. If you anchor your passion with follow-up, key relationship-building skills and an organizational system that really works, you will create an environment in which your business can truly flourish.

Your Mindset—Getting Your Head Right

How your clients see your business begins with how they see you. If you are in your business only for the money, you will come across as needy and greedy. To survive—and thrive—in direct selling, let others see your confidence in your product along with your personal passion for helping people. Believe in your product and no matter what happens, the strength of your belief will keep you on the path to success.

Let the sales process be natural and enjoyable for you and your prospect. Take a deep breath and allow your prospect to digest your information so that it makes sense for her, letting her be a part of the sale. When a person feels included in something, she takes ownership in that process. Enjoy the conversation and let your prospect add to your mission. Allow her to tell you why she needs your product. Share information and turn the sale into a conversation—*she will wind up selling herself.*

Even though she may not buy from you immediately, as long as you stay in touch with her she will eventually buy from you. In the meantime, she will send new customers your way.

If you sell jewelry and a special occasion comes up, she will think of you and your merchandise. If you sell health products, a new health challenge or a new commitment to being healthier will trigger her to think about you. If you sell cosmetics and she wants a new look, you will be first in her thoughts. Even if you are selling legal plans, financial plans or insurance plans—when she has need, she will buy from you.

When you have built the relationship well, then whatever you are selling, your prospect will buy from you when she is ready to make a buying decision. Your job is to stay in touch with her in a positive and persistent way.

Remember that people hate to feel as if you are trying to sell to them. But people love to be educated and to learn about solutions and products that make life easier or more enjoyable. Your role is to share and educate.

Four Ways to Keep the Doors Open for Future Business

- Ask, "May I stay in touch with you?" This is the face-to-face version of email permission marketing.
- Send handwritten thank-you notes.
- Send holiday cards to every prospect.

- Compliment your prospect and make her feel good. You will stay in her memory in a recurring and positive way.

Sharing Your Products and Educating Your Clients

If you believe in what you sell, then you are naturally excited and can't wait for everyone to buy your products or have an opportunity to create additional income. You know how much it will benefit people's lives. You believe in what you are selling so much that you just can't imagine anyone saying no to you. While you understand that the opportunity may not be for everyone, *your products make such good sense!*

But if your product is great, and your prospect receives it positively, why doesn't she buy immediately?

Two Big Factors to Understand

1. A prospect typically requires five to seven exposures—sometimes more—before she buys.

2. No's are not personal—this is business.

You may have to follow up with some prospects many times, and this can go on for a year or longer. You may feel fed up with your prospect and want to throw away her information—*don't!*

Successful leaders never throw away a number until they receive a firm "not interested." Unless the prospect clearly says "no," you should stay in touch. Success never happens without sufficient prospects in your sales funnel.

Anticipate the Emotional Rollercoaster

When you are on a rollercoaster, you are scared, excited and your adrenalin is pumping. The ride goes high and low, up and down.

The same concept happens in your business, starting with the first exposure. Prospects are receptive to you—you feel high. You follow up with a prospect to close the sale and she says, "Call back." Now your excitement has turned into disappointment. You feel low—you thought you were about to close the sale. Then another prospect gives you the thumbs up, buys from you or becomes part of your team. You are excited again, and it lasts until you follow up with the next person who is not ready to respond and asks you to call back.

You are on a rollercoaster. Your emotions go high then low; up and then down. But put yourself in your client's shoes. Life is unpredictable. Since your first exposure, your prospect may have had something come up causing her to hold off on her decision to buy.

As a professional, it is critical that you understand and anticipate the rollercoaster because your voice always reveals whatever emotion you are feeling. Assume the sale, but be ready to accept that it might not happen when you want it to happen.

Your long-term success depends upon you staying in the middle, neither too high nor too low. Understanding this gives you the mindset to overcome your obstacles.

Get Organized for Follow-Up

Two three-ring binders provide a simple and effective way to improve your organization.

- Binder #1 is for the days of the month (thirty-one dividers).
- Binder #2 is for the months of the year (twelve dividers).

In your binders, add one clear sleeve per day or month (to hold loose business cards and notes), with contact sheets for each prospect, positioned between every divider. Starting with the first exposure to a prospect, write down all the information about him or her. Forget depending on your memory!

Make it a practice to ask for business cards from every prospect and to carry blank index cards with you in your portable office. Staple the index card and the business card with the following information onto an individual contact sheet:

- The prospect's name
- Her address
- The date of your first meeting
- Your scheduled follow-up date and time
- Where you met her
- What your prospect was doing when you met
- If you were able to help her, what did you do?
- Were her children with her?
- Was she sick?
- Did you compliment her? What did you say?
- Additional notes and anything else about the meeting

Everything you can find out about your prospect helps you prepare for a friendly follow-up call and building a relationship. When you are speaking with your prospect, you'll want the call to be all about her and the only way to do this is by having your notes—your cheat sheet—at hand.

Know the Right Number of Exposures for Your Business

The key is to work your direct sales business regularly and consistently. When you are working your business part-time, do at least two or three follow-up exposures per day. If you work your business full-time, commit to five to ten follow-up exposures per day. Human nature allows us to tell ourselves we will make up tomorrow the exposures we don't do today—but this is simply not true.

If you do not do a sufficient number of exposures, you will fall short and have challenges. You won't be filling your sales funnel and you will be calling the same people over and over again. You will start to wonder why your prospects no longer give you the time of day and why they run from you. They will stop answering your calls; they will see you and suddenly be "in a hurry." You will be at a party with them and will feel as if they are avoiding you—*and you'll be right*. Focus too much on too few prospects and they will begin to think of you as their stalker.

So stop the insanity. When you see a prospect with whom you are at risk of over-engaging, just be yourself. When she asks you how you are, tell her you are fantastic, business is booming and then drop the subject of business and carry on a purely social conversation. She may bring up business again, but don't you do it.
There is a time for business and a time for just being you. Yes, you want to expose everyone to your business and let them all know what you are doing. However, remember that the key is to fill your sales funnel and follow up when they invite it.

If you keep trying to sell to people who are not ready to be sold, you will wind up feeling rejected, disappointed, discouraged and even a little angry. Unless they tell you to "stop calling" or just say "no," put them in your monthly binder and call them periodically.

In the meantime, expose your business like crazy to new people. I live by this rule: if you are within three feet of me, you are getting a smile, a compliment and a pitch. I talk to people about my business all the time, no matter where I am—gas stations, malls, grocery stores, banks, the post office, parks—*everywhere!*

And because you can engage with a prospect anywhere and anytime, you'll want to always have something about you and your business with you. You never know when you are going to meet your next customer. I also make an effort to shop where others support my business. Business owners understand the philosophy that "people follow their dollars."

Be Willing to Make Cold Calls

Do not be afraid of cold calls. A cold call is nothing more than an open door to a new friend. If you are cold calling on a business in person, enter the business, walk around as if you are browsing and perhaps even buy something to show that you are now a customer. Ask for the owner or manager's name after you make your purchase. Compliment the store and introduce yourself with a big smile and warm handshake, saying something like this:

"Hi (store owner's name), I'm (your name). I love your store. I know so many people I will send your way. You're awesome! By the way, I just wanted to share with you what I do in case you or someone you know is in need of (your products)." Then share briefly about your products and ask, "Can I grab your business card and stay in touch? Thanks _____, see you later. Have a great day."

Be Persistent and Respectful

Any time you introduce your product to a new prospect, you will want to ask to follow up within 48 hours. Make sure you arrange the follow-up time to fit your own schedule. If the prospect asks you to call back at 2PM and you are working and miss the call, then you have lost credibility. Always call when you say you are going to call.

Before you begin each follow-up call, identify how your prospect will benefit from your products and modify your conversation accordingly. When you call, keep the conversation light and friendly. People are busy and you only have seconds to pique their interest. As long as you are pleasant, friendly and not pushy, and you know how to just drip on them, giving them just a little more information to keep their interest each time you speak to them about your business, it will work out very well.

Try starting each call like this:

"Hi, (prospect's first name), it's (your first name). How's your day going? I really appreciate your time and value your feedback. I think you're amazing." Now use the information you collected when you first met her:

- *"How are you feeling?"*
- *"How are your children?"*
- *"Did you find what you were looking for Sunday at the mall?"*

"It was really great meeting you. You made my day on _____; just your smile helped me that day. I wanted to say thank you!" Always find a way to compliment them. People love compliments and they aren't used to getting them.

"You asked me to call you today, is this a good time to talk?" If it's not a good time, say, *"No problem—just a quick question—did you get a chance to look over (your product)?"* If the answer is yes, then ask what she liked best and agree with whatever she says by saying, *"Wow, this is exactly what I saw, too!"* Take the conversation to the next step, and then say, *"May I call you back on (dates and times you are available, giving them a choice of two times)? Thanks _____, have a great day!"*

If the prospect isn't prepared to talk now, remind her that you wouldn't be following up with her if you didn't think this was something beneficial for her. Ask, *"Do you think you will have a chance to look over my brochure within the next day or this week? May I call you back (again giving a choice of times)? Thanks _____, have a great day!"*

Your next call will be the same, only you will use new information based on your last interaction. If you call and there is no answer, leave a light and friendly message: *"Hi (prospect's, first name), it's (your first name), just trying to get in touch with you. Please call me back at* _____. *Talk to you later."*

Try this tip: Call again the next day, but call at a different time and from a different phone. Your prospect won't recognize the number and may answer out of curiosity. If you call from your regular number and she isn't ready to do business with you, she might just let it go to voicemail.

If your third attempt for a call fails, remember, your prospect has your contact information. Put her in your second binder and call again in a month. In the meantime, mail her a cute card just to say "Hi" and to make her smile.

Lastly—and this is very important—when you do interact with the prospect again, there is only one question to ask about the material she has now seen, *"What did you like best?"*

The only question to ask is the positive question. A positive question elicits a positive answer.

Avoid asking for an opinion or what she thinks. These are loaded questions and open the way for a negative response. These questions hurt you in the long run.

Knowing how hard to push is a skill. At the same time, you can't let a good prospect slip through your fingers. Find a place of balance. Practice the ideas we have discussed here consistently and you will find that your follow-up and your overall direct selling effectiveness will be strengthened and your dreams realized.

LYN-DEE ELDRIDGE, CPC, CPMC
Motivational Speaker,
Transformational Coach, Author

Stop the insanity...
change things in your life, for your life

(603) 497-2439
info@lyn-dee.com
www.lyn-dee.com

Lyn-Dee lives in beautiful New Hampshire with her husband, four children and granddaughter. When she is not spending quality time with her family, she is out sharing her inspiring spirit, and truly loves every minute of it. For Lyn-Dee, life is good, but it hasn't always been that way.

The game of life has taken Lyn-Dee from the very bottom to the top. Along the way, she's learned the rules of the game and what it takes to be a winner. Her diverse background has provided her with the experience she uses today to help millions overcome adversity and experience triumphant success of their own.

With a passion and mission for paying it forward by helping others find the greatness within, Lyn-Dee has written several books, such as *Tears of Fears Behind Closed Doors*, published by Mastermind Publishing, LLC in 2008. These books inspire and teach everyone how to have no regrets or not hold grudges, but to appreciate everything that's made you the stronger, wiser person you are today.

Lyn-Dee's drive to empower others is a gift and it's powerful and contagious! Stay connected to Lyn-Dee and spread your wings!

Change How You Think About Recruiting
The Key to Team Growth

By Shari Hudspeth

Recruiting is your path to a six-figure income. Not only will recruiting bring you financial rewards, it's also the most rewarding part of this business.

Once you start recruiting and seeing your new recruits' success, you will feel an intense sense of pride and a new excitement for the business that wasn't there before. It will quickly become your favorite part of your business.

Change Your Mental Picture

So what stops us from recruiting? Our perceptions. Recruiting is easy when you change the way you think about it. A common perception about recruiting is that you have to be pushy. Let me put your mind at ease. Being pushy is not effective. In fact, it doesn't work at all. People resist—and resent—pushy people.

Here are four thoughts that really helped me change my perception about recruiting:

1. *"You can get anything you want out of life if you just help enough other people get what they want."* —Zig Ziglar, Self-help author and speaker.

2. Recruiting is simply sharing something you believe in with someone who will benefit from it. When you recruit someone into the business, you both win.

Do you believe in what you're doing? Have you and your family benefited from your business? Are you happier? Has your business relieved some financial pressure? Have you grown personally as a result of your business? Are there others who would enjoy or need those same benefits?

3. Focus on your prospect. If we can forget about the benefit to us, and really focus on the benefit to others, it's so much easier for us to recruit. Sometimes, just the idea that we get something for recruiting hinders us. When we get totally focused on them, it's mentally much easier for us to recruit.

That means thinking about how your business could benefit them. Do they need extra money? Do they need to get out of the house a couple of nights a week? Do they love to be center stage? Are they naturally inclined to help people?

If you're nervous or afraid to ask, you're focused on the wrong person. Focus on them, and it will be much easier to recruit.

4. Our job is to offer. Their job is to accept or decline. If we don't offer, we've ultimately made the decision for them. I've heard consultants over the years say things like:

"*I didn't ask her because she has three young children.*" "*She makes too much money, she wouldn't be interested.*" "*She's too old.*" "*She's too young.*" "*She's too busy.*" "*She's too shy.*"

We need to let them decide if it's a good choice for their life, not decide for them.

You Never Know Who Is Ready to Join You

When I was a corporate trainer, one of our top-level leaders was a mortgage broker with a six-figure income when someone shared a direct selling opportunity with her and she said yes. Her reason for agreeing was that she was working 80 hours a week as a mortgage broker. She replaced that income quickly and quit the mortgage business.

Another leader was a district attorney who just needed "something fun in her life." One of the ladies on my team was working a full-time job and five part-time jobs when she joined my team. As her income grew, she quit the jobs one by one. Today she is one of the top income earners in her company. Another woman joined my team for the sole purpose of overcoming her shyness.

We never know what our business opportunity can do for someone else. With that said, we can certainly make our offer in a way that makes it appealing, in a way that is more likely to get a "yes." Let me show you what I mean.

Make Your Offer Compelling

Imagine you and your family are out to dinner. You've finished your meal and the server comes by, offers you more coffee and asks if you'd care for any dessert. How likely are you to say, "Yes, I'd love some dessert. What do you have?" Not very likely!

Now imagine that you're out to a restaurant, and as you finish your meal, your server comes by, offers you coffee and says, "Let me tell you about a few of our dessert offerings. We have the best cheesecake in the state. We drizzle a wonderful raspberry puree over it, and then we top it with a touch of whipped cream. Or perhaps you're a chocolate fan. You'll love our chocolate fudge cake. We pour hot fudge over the top and serve it with a scoop of vanilla ice cream. Then there's my personal favorite, our famous apple crisp, with a great crumbled topping and served warm. What do you think? May I bring you a dessert menu, or did I tempt you with one of our specialties?"

Isn't it more tempting to say yes to the second offer? The server painted a picture—he helped us visualize. We could almost taste it. It's the same with recruiting. We don't have to be pushy. Our job is to make the offer; theirs is to accept or decline. However, like the server, we can learn to make our offer in a way that is more appealing, in a way that makes people want to say, "Yes!" You'll find suggestions throughout this chapter to make what you're offering very desirable.

Embrace Hearing No

A big thing that keeps people from recruiting is the fear of hearing no. I once heard someone say, "We would all be successful if it weren't for the fear of rejection." We think when someone says no to us that they are rejecting us. That's not true.

What if you were at a friend's house, and she offered you and her other guests a brownie. Some of the guests said yes, but you said, "No, thank you. I'm on a diet." Were you rejecting her? Of course not. You were just trying to stick to your diet. Others did say yes though, and maybe on another day you would too.

Recruiting is the same. You may offer several people the business opportunity and some will say yes and others will say, "No, thank you." Even though some said no this time, it doesn't mean they won't say yes later. Circumstances change. I asked one of my top leaders to become a consultant five times before she said yes. Today, she earns a six-figure income. We are both glad I kept asking.

When you change the way you think about recruiting, you will change the way you ask, and then you will change your results.

The Very Best Place to Recruit is at Your Parties

There's someone at every party who wants to join your business—they just don't know it yet. The key is to make sure that you go into every party with a recruiting focus. Most of us tend to go into our parties with a sales focus, a hope for bookings and a low focus on recruiting.

At a party you have the entire duration of the event to build excitement and desire around joining your team. How do you make sure you don't miss someone who would benefit from your business opportunity?

One of the best ways to maximize your recruiting success at a party is through excellent host coaching. Effective host coaching equals high attendance, which equals high sales. We do that before the party, so we don't need to focus on sales at the party. With eight to ten guests who place an average order of $50, your party should end up at $400 to $500.

Then, play a booking game *and* place effective booking seeds through-out your presentation, so that with eight to ten guests at your party, you can easily book two or more new parties.

This allows you to go into your parties with one antenna—your recruiting antenna. By just focusing on recruiting, you'll notice things like:

- Someone whose eyes get big when you talk about the income opportunity
- Someone who's crazy about the product
- Someone who gets excited when you talk about the incentive trip

You'll hear clues like:
- "I love to travel."
- "We could use a second car."
- "It's so great to have a break from my toddlers."
- "I had so much fun tonight."

Use your recruiting antenna to pick up on these comments. They're telling you why your business could benefit them.

Three Ways to Respond to the Same Comment

Think about how you might respond to this comment if you had a sales focus at your party:

"I'd love to get that XYZ product, but it's a little out of my budget." You might think, "That's an expensive piece. I need that sale!" And you would immediately begin to tell her all the benefits of that product.

If you went into the party with a booking focus, and you heard the same comment you might think, "She should book a party and get it for free." You would share with her how she could earn that incredible piece for free by hosting her own party.

If you went into the party with a recruiting focus and heard the same comment you might think, "If it's out of her budget, she might be able to use some extra income." You could say something like, "I don't know if this is anything you'd be interested in, but I'd love to share with you a fun way to increase your monthly income. Would you like to take home some information?"

Depending on our focus, we will hear and respond differently to customer comments. The first key to being a consistent recruiter is to go into your parties with one antenna—your recruiting antenna.

Plant Recruiting Seeds

Seeds are not direct thought provokers like, "Watch what I do tonight and see how easy it is." Those are good too. A recruiting seed is so subtle they don't even know they heard it.

A recruiting seed might sound like this: *"I'm going to give you ladies an extra ticket for the drawing tonight just because you're so fun! I love getting out and visiting with great women a couple of times a week, but you are an extra fun group."* Consciously they hear that they were an "extra fun group," but the hidden seed is that you get out a couple of times a week.

Another recruiting seed might be, *"This is one of my favorite products. It came in my first kit five years ago and I still bring it to every party."* They consciously hear that that's one of your favorite products, but the subtle seed is that you get a kit as a consultant, with lots of fun things in it.

Seeds build desire, but they need to be scripted and practiced. You don't want to count on them just popping into your head during your presentation.

Pre-Plan Your Personal Commercial

Sharing your personal commercial midway through your party is a great way to add desire to becoming a consultant. It should be short—about three minutes or less—and should share four key messages.

1. What attracted you to the business
2. What you were nervous about before you started
3. How your life is better
4. What you love most about your business today

183

When we only talk about one aspect there may be only one person in the room who could relate. For instance if you said, *"I got started in this business just to get out of the house once a week,"* there may be only one person in the room who resonates with that message. By speaking to four different aspects, most people in the room can relate to at least one of them.

Your commercial could sound like this:

"I got started with (your company) *just to earn enough money to buy new living room furniture. I was so nervous that I wouldn't get any bookings. I was surprised that I earned enough money in two months to buy the furniture and still had eight more bookings! That was a year ago. Thanks to my business, we have lots of little extras we didn't have before, like a debt-free Christmas and long weekend vacations, and I can treat myself to things like a pedicure without feeling guilty. I think my favorite part is all the new friends I've made: my hostesses and customers, and the other consultants who really helped me to learn how to do this."*

Play the Question Game

Follow your personal commercial with a short question/answer time. You could give raffle tickets for a small prize if they asked you a question. A question and answer time works so well because we aren't standing up front in lecture mode telling them everything we love about our business. They're asking questions and we're simply answering them. It's an easier way for them to take in the information.

However, if you just say, *"Okay, this is your opportunity to ask me anything about my business,"* you'll have a long, uncomfortable silence. You have to give them starter questions to get the conversation going, and then they will get so involved that you'll have to stop or it will go on forever.

To get it started, you can say something like this:

"Okay! It's question time. This is your opportunity to ask me anything you want to about my business. It has to be about my business. You can't ask how old I am, but you can ask me about our incentive trip to Hawaii, our $1000 bonus, how much I earn, or how much it costs to get started. For every question you ask, I will give you a ticket, and at the end of the question and answer period we'll draw for a prize. Who wants to go first?"

Of course, the starter questions are the first ones they ask, so I made sure they were the ones I wanted them to ask. At the end of your question and answer time, wrap it up with a group offer to join the business.

A group offer could sound like this:

"I hope this question and answer time gave some of you food for thought. You can try the business for a few weeks and see what you think. There's really nothing to lose. If you like it, you'll have a great business going. If you don't, you can quit. It's really that simple. The worst thing that can happen is you earned some extra money and got a lot of great products in your kit."

When my team started using that verbiage, our recruiting went up 70 percent in one month and our team sales doubled the next month. Words like "career" or "start a business" can make people nervous. They sound like a long-term commitment or make people think there's a big investment. "Try it for three weeks," says it's on a trial basis. The bottom line is that signing up means they are going to try it for a short time and see if they like it anyway. You just made it easier to say yes to giving it a try.

Apply the ideas in this chapter and watch your recruiting flourish. Then share these ideas with your team and watch everyone flourish. Ongoing recruiting is the key to building a successful team.

SHARI HUDSPETH
Average to Excellence, LLC

The path from average to excellence for direct selling professionals

(253) 630-2406
shari@averagetoexcellence.com
www.averagetoexcellence.com

Shari has over 24 years experience in the direct sales industry. She spent 11 of those years in the field, and 13 as a corporate trainer, home office executive, and as the founder and President of her own speaking, training and coaching business.

Her results include building a $14 million organization with 140 leaders in just six years. Six of those leaders reached the top level of leadership earning a six-figure income. Shari also took a start-up company from just four leaders to 38 in 18 months.

Working for six different companies, she has acquired skills, ideas and successful tools from many home office executives and top-level leaders that she can pass on to you.

Having been in the field as recently as 2000-2005, holding 150-175 parties a year personally, Shari's cutting-edge training shows that she understands that today's customers, hostesses, consultants and leaders are very different than they were even a decade ago.

Shari prides herself on not just being a motivational speaker, but a motivational teacher, always providing a step-by-step plan to help you achieve your dreams and goals!

Recruiting High Net Worth and Highly Influential People

By Lorna Rasmussen

She moves with grace across the crowded room. Dressed in designer clothes, with perfect hair and makeup, she is the quintessence of sophistication and wealth. All eyes are on her and everyone seems to either know her—or want to. She is chic, sophisticated and is, obviously, the person to know. She is the *Networking Diva.*

He stands in the center of a small group of very attentive and smart-looking people. They hang on his every word. Others are constantly joining the small group, pressing forward just to be in his presence and hear what he has to say. They bring others up to meet him, introducing him as if it is a privilege just to shake his hand. He is the *Very Influential Person.*

She just sparkles. The room lights up as she enters and people are drawn to her like moths to a light. There is a joy about her and everyone seems affected and infected by it. She is the *Social Butterfly.*

Standing at a social gathering or a networking function or watching from the sidelines at a business meeting, you would think that these are the people to meet. These are the people you would love to talk to about your direct sales business. They would be marvelous at it. They would make you a lot of money—if only you knew how to meet them, how to introduce them to your business, how to recruit them.

The Quest to "Recruit Up"

If you have been in direct sales or network marketing for even a few weeks, you likely were told to "recruit up." It is a standard practice in direct sales companies to teach this concept to new recruits who are probably baffled by what it means, as well as by how to do it. What most people mean by "recruit up" is to recruit individuals who make more money, have more influence or are in a more socially elevated position in life than you are. They are the prized prospects for our businesses because they either know a lot of people like our "Networking Diva," or people are attracted to them like our "Social Butterfly" or they have information and influence like our "VIP."

They may also have a great Rolodex® (database) and can pick up the phone and connect you with people you couldn't dream of meeting. They have resources and often understand the idea of spending money to make money. They are willing to play big: they do big deals, charge a lot for their services and have an affluent clientele. They are often risk takers—willing to try new things, not easily intimidated and often inventive. They are usually highly intelligent, competitive and confident. They will be successful at just about anything they put their minds to. They could take your business and explode it in weeks or even days.

So how do you find them, meet them and, more importantly, how do you get them to look at a direct sales opportunity?

Where to Find High Net Worth/High Influence (HNW/HI) Prospects

The world is full of high net worth individuals. Some of them realize they are working too hard, some of them hate their work, and some of them are tired of working for someone else. Some of these very professional, highly educated individuals are today out looking for employment that matches their former job in terms of salary and perks. You can find them sitting next to you on a plane, at Little League games, at church and in civic associations. They network, just like you do, at chambers of commerce, business associations and civic groups. This is especially true if they are job hunting, as they know that the best jobs are found through networking, not ads.

High net worth individuals also belong to private business and dinner clubs and alumni organizations, and they are often involved in charity work. If they have businesses, they may belong to professional associations that support their businesses, such as the AIA for architects or CPA societies or the American Medical Association. They may be part of organizations that provide them with continuing education or they may simply join groups associated with a hobby or an interest. In America, if four people have an interest in something they form a club or organization. We are joiners and our HNW/HI prospects are as well.

How to Approach HNW/HI Prospects

Direct selling associates come up to me all the time and say, "I'm trying to recruit a doctor, or a lawyer, or a very wealthy individual. What do I say to them, how do I approach them?" First, you approach them as you would anyone, which is to follow the Golden Rule. Approach people like you would like to be approached. In a social gathering or a networking meeting, it is important to approach people with a "be of service attitude." How can you help this person? Well, first you need to know about them. Everyone—I mean everyone—loves to talk about themselves.

189

I'm not suggesting that you approach a Ted Turner and ask him how he feels about Time Warner taking over CNN. Keep your initial contact with the person on a neutral subject. If you know anything about a person's favorite charity, their favorite sport or hobby, start there. If you don't know them, ask open-ended questions that will start the ball rolling. Some examples are: "How do you know the host/hostess?" or "Is this the first time you've attended one of these meetings?" or compliment them on something. "I love your tie. Did you choose it to go with that suit because it certainly goes well."

Once you are engaged in conversation, listen very carefully to what they are saying and don't be thinking about how to squeeze in something about yourself. Watch them as well; their body language is as important as what they are saying. Don't pry into personal areas but look for common ground. If they mention that their kids are into sports and you have a child who plays, go down that road. Remember to focus on them. Telling them your stories does not engage them. Simply look for ways to connect the two of you and let them talk. If you are at a business meeting, you might ask them about their business and find out who would be a great customer for them. Maybe you know of other places where they can meet those prospective customers. Look for ways to help them rather than ways to impress them.

How to Attract HNW/HI Prospects

The goal is to attract these prospects to you. How do you become someone they want to know? Certainly, as discussed in the previous section, being of worth and value to them is key. It is also who you are as an individual. But, you might say, I can't dress like the Networking Diva or expound on current topics like the VIP. How do I attract these people? One way is to work on yourself. My mentors have always told me, "To have you must first be." In other words, being self-confident, being of service, being focused and being authentic are all ways to make you an attractive person. Dress, information and sparkle will come as you become more comfortable with who you are and become more successful.

The most difficult transition we all make is to "be" before we "become." A couple of hints are to read and listen to personal development material, to practice doing affirmations and to "act as if." The latter is perhaps the most important. It is hard to act confident—shoulders thrown back, smile on your face and a firm handshake—and not feel confident. Someone who exudes confidence, is comfortable in their own skin and is interested in the other person, is a very attractive individual–and someone that anyone would love to meet.

How to Introduce and Attract HNW/HI Prospects to Direct Sales

Now you are comfortable meeting these prospects, you've learned to engage them and you feel that you are ready to introduce them to your business opportunity. How do you bring up the subject? The first thing I would ask you is, "How do you feel about your business?" I have met a lot of people active in direct sales who are not themselves completely sold on the concept. They think of it as something they are doing until something real comes along, until they get a good job or until they come up with an idea for a real business. If you are not 100 percent sold on the fact that your business opportunity is the best and that direct sales is a great option for people, you will never attract people to your business, whether they are HNW/HI or not.

What you think matters more than anything else. The first sale you will ever make is to yourself. I am sold on direct sales. I don't believe that there is anything else out there that can compete with the opportunity to work for a first class direct sales company. I know that it is, for the right person, one of the best ways to make money and have a life. It can create an incredible lifestyle and give a person something that people rarely have—money and the time to enjoy it. I have met doctors, lawyers, business people and professionals from every field who are happier and more fulfilled by working in direct selling than they were in their professions. Because I know these people, know these stories and have experienced it myself, there is no doubt in my mind that everyone should at least be open to looking at the opportunity.

But you might be saying, "I don't know that first hand." It is great to have your own personal experiences and if you don't yet, go meet successful direct sales professionals, read about them, join organizations like the Direct Selling Women's Alliance and learn through them. Belief in the profession of direct sales, belief in your own company and belief in yourself are the prerequisites for approaching people with confidence and certainty. When you do that, they will listen. It need not take you being personally successful to feel this way. But you do need to know about others. There is an adage in sales that "Facts tell and stories sell." When approaching a prospect, be filled with stories about people just like them who changed their lives by being associated with your company. Attend your company's meetings and conventions, listen to conference calls and read about success stories. Use those stories as your own when talking to your prospects. "A woman in our company was a doctor just like you, then..."

Remember the Law of Duplication

The natural tendency is to do something different with different people when approaching them. I have always treated people the same—in terms of the process. If I give prospects a DVD, put them on a call with an expert and take them to a meeting—that's what I do with my HNW/HI prospects. Why? Because if I treat them differently, they will never learn how the system works to bring other prospects into the system. If there is a system for recruiting, everyone should go through that system or you are violating the first tenet of the system—that it is a system.

I will now add that you should treat everyone uniquely, because each person is special in his or her experiences and background. You put them through the system but you acknowledge their distinctiveness within that system. If they have had years of hiring people as a top manager in a corporation, you recognize that experience and show them how it works in our profession. Direct sales is different because we aren't hiring people, we are recruiting a voluntary army. You acknowledge their years of expertise and you don't treat them as if they have never done something like this before. However, you help them shape their background experience to work in this new profession.

Treating people uniquely really begins with listening to them and acknowledging them. They are accomplished individuals, and they are also new to this direct selling world. There is not, for example, a direct correlation between running a national sales team in a Fortune 1000 company and running a voluntary army of recruits in a direct sales company.

Keep Them in the Business Long Enough to Succeed

Success is a must for highly successful people. It is a challenge for them to start over in something where they feel they are floundering. The biggest challenge is the feeling they have of not succeeding fast enough. This is particularly true when they see others, less skilled or accomplished, becoming more successful faster than them. The important thing to do is to redefine success for them. Be constantly vigilant when they use markers from their old life to define success in this new profession. In their old profession they got fired for not being immediately successful. In this profession it is understood and accepted. In fact, in many direct sales companies you may never be asked to "act the expert" unless you are on a three-way call or speaking from the stage. As a top-ranking individual in my company, when I am recruiting I do exactly the same things I did years ago as a new person in the business. I use tools, three-way calls and meetings to recruit my associates. The only time my prospects will hear me do the whole presentation is when I do it from the stage or in a meeting. I want them to know they only have to do with their prospects what I did with them. For many of our HNW/HI people this is a complete paradigm change. They are no longer expected to act as the expert but rather to act as the messenger of the expert information. That's why people with few skills and little experience can do as well and better than those with lots of skills—they don't expect or want to be experts. Unless our HNW/HI individuals understand this concept, they will feel frustrated and quit.

Understand that, in the end, whoever your recruits are, your attitude toward them will also color their experience. This is a business of duplication. It is an easy business that requires people to do simple, easily-duplicated things, over and over. Showing people the system, teaching them to duplicate the system and believing in the profession is key to the success of your business. HNW/HI individuals are just one component of a successful business.

Use the ideas shared above to recruit HNW/HI prospects. Remember, they are just like everyone else—they put their pants on one leg at a time. Be confident, be professional and put your full attention on them—not you. Ask interested questions, follow your recruiting system, and you may be surprised at who wants to join your team.

LORNA RASMUSSEN
The Absolute Best Way

(404) 814-0342
lorna@absolutebestway.com
www.absolutebestway.com

Lorna's career in direct selling spans fifteen years. Tenacity and determination played an important role in her success, but so did the teachings of a man by the name of Paul J. Meyer, who taught her goal setting and helped her develop self-confidence. For the past eleven years she has earned a six-figure annual income. "When I lost my house to a fire four years ago, I didn't work on my business for almost a year and then only part-time for the next four years. Because of the team I had created, I saw only a small decline in my business."

Lorna is sold on direct sales as the answer for work/life balance in the lives of women. To share her love of the profession and the information that made her successful, Lorna began writing books on the subject. Two books in a series have been published in 2009: *The Absolute Best Way for You to Make Money* and a similar book focusing on African American women. Both are available on her website.

She has a son, Drew, and lives with her husband, architect George Hornbein, in Atlanta, Georgia.

Communicating for Positive Team Results

By Gale Bates

"A leader's greatest obligation is to make possible
an environment where people can aspire to change the world."
—Carly Fiorina, former CEO, Hewlett-Packard

One of the greatest things about direct sales is learning how to grow a profitable business and grow yourself along the way at the same time. We actively hold parties and interact with fun and interesting customers. We book future parties and build relationships with delightful and fun hostesses, and we recruit new consultants, supporting and guiding them on a path to success. Once we build a team, we become part of a leadership group and enjoy extra benefits and rewards.

Successful selling, booking, recruiting and leadership are all rooted in effective communication. As a leader, my purpose and commitment was to empower women to build successful and profitable businesses. I quickly realized that the common bond in recognizing each individual's success was through using effective, positive communication. Affirming each person's successes through multiple channels of communication added to that common bond, and I found inspiring and motivating messages were the catalyst in helping women become more confident and have increased self esteem. When everyone interacts through positive communication and becomes connected through the common bond of achievement, the team and everyone on it become unstoppable.

What's important is to be very clear about what inspires you. What is your commitment and passion regarding helping others? When you are clear about your mission and convey the abundance available through direct sales to others in a positive manner, you can have a significant role in changing people's lives.

Be Open to Communication

I recall one beautiful Saturday summer evening in Denver, Colorado. I was relaxing after dinner when my phone rang. A cascade of energy burst through the phone, *"Gale, I did it! I am a National Incentive Winner! I'm on my way home and my party was over $2000 in sales. I got three bookings and the hostess is thinking about joining my team. I am so, so excited I am a winner!"*

This was a special moment. It was an awesome moment for a consultant in my group sharing her great success, and it was a moment in my life when I knew I was building success in others. I wouldn't have missed this for the world, and that moment was available because of my open-door communication policy.

Communicating your availability as a leader is the first step to creating respectful relationships. I created an open-door policy that helped people understand I was available *when needed*. It is important to be clear about your expectations in communicating with your field, and it is important your field is clear on how to respond to those expectations.

Communicating with Positive Interaction

There are many ways to communicate. It all boils down to the words we use and the tone of voice that makes a difference in helping people feel good. A way to build someone's self worth is to praise and recognize her natural strengths. When you use positive, uplifting and encouraging words, you develop strong connections. Strong connections lead to lasting friendships and a sense of belonging. People stay when they feel like they belong. People excel when you value their strengths. The whole team succeeds when you create an inspiring and uplifting environment in which to work. John Maxwell, leadership expert and author says, *"Communication increases commitment and connection, which in turn fuels action."*

We are living in the age of communication. It is possible to be connected in an instant, either online or offline, like never before. Communication is one of the most powerful tools used in marketing, selling and spreading news. It is a critical part of your business strategy in selling to customers, coaching hostesses and building leaders.

The following nine communication tools provide a solid foundation for building a flourishing direct sales business, and will put you in the spotlight as a positive, caring and successful leader.

1. Build Community through Telephone Communication

The 80/20 rule applies to most areas of our business. If you read my chapter in *Build It BIG: 101 Secrets From Top Direct Selling Experts*, published by Dearborn Trade Publishing in 2005, you will remember Vilfredo Pareto. In 1906, Italian economist Vilfredo Pareto created a mathematical formula describing the unequal distribution of wealth in his country. He observed that 20 percent of the people owned 80 percent of the wealth. This has become known as Pareto's Principle, or the 80/20 rule.

Applying this principle to your team, you will find that 20 percent of your people usually do 80 percent of the sales and recruiting on a consistent basis. Therefore, it's extremely important to communicate with your 20 percent regularly. One of the most successful communication systems that I initiated as my team moved to the number one position in the country were my Talk10™ Calls. These were 10-minute weekly calls made available to team members who wanted fast growth and were aligned with our mission to empower women.

Talk10 Calls have strict rules:
• The call only lasts 10 minutes—hence the name Talk10.
• She calls you, the leader—this makes her accountable.
• The talk is only business—no personal chitchat.
• You can only miss one call, or you are out—personal accountability.
• The call always ends with a definite call to action.

The value of this communication method was in the results. The women on my team who took advantage of this communication tool were the ones who moved up in the company and received numerous awards. Witnessing the amazing transformation of these women as they walked across the stage to receive their awards was truly exhilarating. These were ordinary women who had learned how to become extraordinary.

2. Embrace Hotlines and Podcast Communications

Have you ever felt like you were running in place and not getting anywhere and needed some kind of direction? Do you ever have a day when you just want to curl up in bed and not face the day because you need a word of inspiration? What if you could tap into a wealth of ideas and information once a day that would motivate you to take action, or even to jump out of your comfort zone?

A powerful way to send positive messages every day with hot tips that motivate and help people succeed is by creating a daily or weekly hotline or podcast system. This style of communication instills confidence as well as knowledge, and the benefits of blasting up-to-the-minute messages or hot ideas with enthusiasm and passion keep consultants engaged on their own success path.

A hotline is a daily five-minute telephone message created through voice messaging. A podcast is a simple audio message created on your website that can be played on someone's computer or downloaded to an mp3 player or iPod®. Quick, empowering messages allow you to:
• Break down specific areas of selling, like how to be an expert order taker, or tips on how to have a $1000 party
• Provide compelling telephone scripts on increasing bookings
• Role-play and teach the fine art of interviewing and recruiting
• Share amazing stories on how to give the best customer care
• Stimulate people with motivating messages on success

Create a theme and use books like *Direct Selling Power* or *Build It BIG* as resources for your messages. Another great thing you can do with this type of communication is give praise and recognition. I loved using this method to share first successes. It was so effective for building confidence and enthusiasm in my team members.

3. Capitalize on Teleconference Training
A very popular way to communicate and teach business-building tools is through teleclass training. If you need visuals for your training, do a webinar. In teleconference training, whether just audio or complete with visuals, you're able to structure a fun, uplifting and rewarding learning experience. Just like your local meetings, you can enroll top performers to deliver a specific training component and empower belief in others by highlighting their strengths.

Another extremely effective way to communicate through the telephone is by using three-way calling technology. Facilitating three-way calls with consultants and their business prospects had a huge impact on building a massive recruiting culture in my team.

Telephone communication is a key business development tool that can be easily used to disseminate positive messages, stay connected to everyone and build community. It is essential to you and your team's success.

4. Connect through Online Communication

For many, email communication is the preferred manner of communicating in today's world. We find it fast and effective while providing a written record and often, quick results. Aside from individual emails, a professional way to communicate strong, positive and timely messages to your team is to use a database management and email sending service like Constant Contact®, iContact® or AWeber®. You can add photos or pictures to add interest and emotion to your message, and you can choose a specific template that supports your message with a theme. Your company may also have online templates and email systems that you can use.

Sending online ezines and blog messages to customers and team members can be a very efficient way to enhance relationships. These online email services offer fantastic tracking reports that allow you to see who's reading the emails. You might notice a team member who is not opening emails and all she needs is a personal telephone call of support to help her get back on track.

If you're blasting an important message via email, keep the content short and to the point. Nothing is more annoying than having to scan down a long email with lots of wording. Make the subject heading interesting and significant. If it's simply a "Message from Gale," it might not get opened. Use direct words in the subject line, like

"Express Message", "Read ASAP re: sales incentive" or "Special Offer from Gale."

5. Become Savvy about Social Media

People around the world are more connected than ever before. Social media allows you to have a huge impact on inspiring others. It can also build your credibility and reputation as a professional.

All communication you send using Facebook®, Twitter® or LinkedIn® should have professional, positive content. It has the same "know, like and trust" factor as offline networking. Once you build the trust, they will be interested in your product and want to do business.

Write positive content about the benefits of your product, your lifestyle and your hobbies and let people get to know you. Look at what might be missing in the marketplace where your product would fill the gap. Be of service to your customers and hostesses. Integrating social networking into your customer care system is the key to receiving online recommendations and referrals.

Congratulate a team member online; show others how praise and recognition are a vital part of our industry. Share ideas you learned at a meeting, or ideas you taught at your meeting. Joyful team interaction online sends messages to others who might want to be part of the synergy and join your team. For more information on building Your business through social media, read Karen Clark's chapter on page 89 entitled *Building an Online Presence for your Direct Sales Business*.

6. Be Seen Using Video Communications

The latest high-tech wave of communicating for positive results is through video. I view this new communication method as similar to making a first impression. On video, people are appraising your visual and behavioral appearance as well as your voice and tone. They are observing your demeanor, mannerisms and body language and even assessing what you're wearing. Within the first five seconds of your video, you can make an indelible impression and become more memorable as a professional direct seller.

Video conferencing comprises another new wave of team building. If you have a team scattered across the country, using this method of training helps build stronger team connections and instills confidence in team members who have no support in their area.

Online communication is part of our everyday world. Be aware of the amount of time you spend communicating online. Our business is all about time allocation and evaluating those high-revenue-producing activities.

7. Communicate through the Power of the Printed Word

Seeing your name in print reinforces every other form of communication from an announcement at a meeting or a telephone call, to a handshake or a hug for a job well done. People *love* to see their name in print.

The power of the printed word validates the praise because it's a solid piece of evidence to share with others. When a person shares the printed material highlighting their exciting achievements, the encouraging feedback creates enormous positive emotions. It is those positive emotions that drive people to achieve their goals.

Printed newsletters are a proven method of communicating positive content. They are an ideal medium to recognize achievements and spread the benefits of your unique product line. Start with a simple one-page newsletter as a Microsoft Word® document. My first newsletter was called *The Monthly Memo*. I had five team members. I wrote a small intro paragraph and the rest was all about recognizing each person's contribution.

As your team grows, so does your printed newsletter. It may not be cost-effective to have a monthly printed newsletter when you have a large team. When my team grew I sent a weekly online ezine and produced a PDF success newsletter once a quarter. It's important that every newsletter be sent out on a consistent basis. If writing is not your skill, then hire someone to write it for you.

Your newsletter should be easy to read and contain success stories, which not only highlight successful team members, they also solidify your mission to empower women and have a profound influence on others' lives.

8. The Handwritten Word Still Matters

In an era of electronic mail, a handwritten note is a treasured thing. It is also one of the best ways to make someone feel good. Writing a few words of encouragement, support or gratitude in a special note card conveys a very personal touch. It is a marvelous relationship builder, and clearly differentiates you from others. These few words will sometimes make the difference in a team member's confidence and momentum. My top seller sent a handwritten thank-you note to every customer who placed an order. It may be old-fashioned, but the time you spend writing heartfelt words to someone will be well worth it in terms of repeat business and developing solid relationships.

9. Face-to-Face Communication

Today, most business communication occurs by telephone, email and sometimes even snail mail. However, communicating in the same room where someone is speaking and someone is listening is the highest and most multi-faceted form of building relationships and friendships. The signals we offer through our eyes, our body movements and even our appearance all influence the way our words are interpreted.

Your interpersonal skills are extremely important. The success of your business is determined by creating the most positive, memorable experiences for hostesses and customers at your parties, as well as sharing the business opportunity face-to-face. I placed great value on training my team in meeting face-to-face with a business prospect. We called them "coffee chat interviews" where we simply shared information about the business over coffee in a relaxed atmosphere. Holding several face-to-face coffee chat interviews every week is the fastest way to build a team and become a top recruiter in your company.

Also, team building depends heavily on face-to-face communication. I love to say that I built the foundation of my direct selling business around my kitchen table with my first two leaders. We had fun getting to know one another over good food and supporting each other in building strong businesses. It is very fulfilling to be part of a winning team. Attending monthly team meetings and interacting face-to-face while learning important ideas is key to your success. Also know that where we gain the most positive interaction is at national conventions. Meeting people from all over the country or the world expands our own horizons, with the sharing of ideas and positive experiences.

It is virtually impossible to identify any part of a direct sales business that isn't based on communication. The key is to remember the power of the words that we possess. We must always pay attention to our words when we meet a new prospect face-to-face; communicate with customers, hostesses and team members through the telephone; or when we connect online through email, video or social media.

Communicating for positive results is about offering up the right words at the right time through the right method, to promote, encourage and inspire others to greatness—and in the process we inspire ourselves.

Decide which of the above tools you want to start using right away, and watch your direct selling business take off.

GALE BATES
Gale R. Bates, LLC

Your accountability partner

(206) 902-8215
galebates@mymentorbiz.com
www.mymentorbiz.com

Gale Bates, DSWA Certified Coach, is a corporate trainer, author and international business coach in direct sales. Gale partners with corporations and leaders who want to grow and increase their net worth.

Her entrepreneurial journey began with her unique Tutu Nene product line, marketed to museums and stores across the United States, culminating in her own successful Tutu Nene boutiques in Hawaii. Fifteen years ago, she joined the direct selling industry and developed a million-dollar business reaching the #1 position in her company more than once. As a top leader, she created successful selling, sponsoring and coaching techniques that inspire women to achieve their goals.

In 2007, Gale became a solo-entrepreneur, expanding her business internationally in Australia, New Zealand and the United States. She launched MyMentorbiz coaching services and publishes a free bi-monthly newsletter, *MyMentorbiz Bulletin for Direct Sales Entrepreneurs*, helping women grow profitable, successful direct sales businesses.

Gale is a dual citizen of the United States and Australia, married with three grown children. She is a published direct sales industry writer participating in *Build It BIG: 101 Secrets From Top Direct Selling Experts*, published by Dearborn Trade Publishing in 2005 and *Coaching Now*, a CD published by the Direct Selling Women's Alliance in 2009. She is also the author of three published children's books.

Turning New Recruits into Leaders
Eight Simple Strategies to Catapult Results

By Sallie Meshell

A leader stands out by
the nature of her commitment to her team.

In the previous chapters, you have learned strategies to successfully recruit others and develop into a leader yourself. Now is the time to learn how to turn those new balls of enthusiastic energy—your recruits—into future leaders.

Leading a team can be one of the most rewarding experiences of your direct selling career, but many times people struggle with how to actually make this happen. Additionally, most people confuse management with leadership. Managing is directing and controlling, whereas leading is motivating by showing the way.

What kind of leader do you feel you are? How do you think your team would rate you? You may be surprised to learn that most consultants feel as though their upline is not doing a great job. Here is a successful blueprint to implement with your new recruits that will set your team apart and create a group of prosperous leaders.

Discover Her "Why"

First, it is essential to know why she has chosen to be a part of your team. Everyone has a different reason for joining and until you know what that is you cannot truly guide her along her journey. One of the biggest mistakes that a sponsor can make is to assume that your recruit wants to be on the same career path as you. Many very successful direct sellers did not start out considering this as a career on their first day. That concept may not be something a recruit can wrap her mind around in the beginning. She may have limiting beliefs that make her think small. How many times have we heard the proverbial, "I'm just looking to earn a little extra money"? In the beginning, she may just want to buy wholesale or have more social interaction in her life. Most join to make money, but the underlying significance here is that it is not for the money itself—it is for what the money can *do* for them. Once she reveals her material "why," keep asking exploratory questions until you understand her emotional "why."

Your new recruit may tell you that she needs to make $500 per month. The monetary figure is her material "why." However, her emotional "why" is the reason she needs the money. It may be for a car payment, but if you look deeper, she may want to fulfill her dream to be a nurse and need transportation to get to school or a new job. Her emotional "why" will come from her heart, and therefore will be the basis for her actions and the key to sustaining her commitment during times when she feels discouraged.

To find her material "why," ask questions such as:
- *What are your goals for this business?*
- *How much income are you looking to create to feel satisfied with your new business?*

When looking for her emotional "why," ask an exploratory question such as:
- *When you accomplish this goal, what kind of a difference will this income make in your life?*

Understand Communication Styles

Does your new recruit love to be on stage receiving awards or would she prefer a special handwritten letter? During group trainings, does she love to be called on or does she avoid making eye contact in hopes that you will pick someone else? Does she prefer to have all the information at once or will that overwhelm her? Knowing these answers will enable you to more effectively work together, ultimately leading to your mutual success.

Communication is the foundation of relationships. Karen Phelps, direct selling speaker and trainer, surveyed several hundred direct sellers working for 40 different companies. The survey results indicated that 54 percent of polled recruits said their upline needed to improve their communication. Part of the reason this number is so high is because we all communicate in different ways. Think in terms of your teammates: some are quiet, some want to be on stage, some need a checklist and some need to feel in control.

Your leadership and communication styles are heavily influenced by your personality, which affects how you communicate, build relationships, conduct meetings and encourage your team. These differences in communication styles can get in the way of clear communication and understanding.

To inspire action, you must know how your team members best receive communication. This aids you by making the most efficient use of time and serves your recruits by speaking their language. Additionally, if you are not speaking their language, then it is possible that you might even be discouraging them. Once you have a framework for understanding these differences, you can work with your team much more effectively.

A simple, yet powerful, tool for developing this understanding is Dr. Robert Rohm's DiSC® model. Not only will this system help you communicate more effectively, but you will be able to identify and value the key strengths of each of your team members. For a comprehensive discussion on DiSC®, see Cindy Sakai's chapter, *People Smarts*, on page 133.

Create a Blueprint for Success

Did you know that most attrition in direct selling occurs within the first 60–90 days, and that the first 48–72 hours after signing a new recruit are the most critical? Based on Karen Phelps' survey, 51 percent of consultants said their upline does not provide adequate training. When your new recruit first signs up, she is on an emotional high. This is the best time for action. Therefore, creating a blueprint for success with your new recruit will dramatically increase her success rate. Help her create a daily accomplishment list for the first seven days, then weekly for the first month. Continue this through 60 and 90 days and be sure to include sponsoring within the first 30 days, which will instill a commitment to stay in the business.

Creating and maintaining this plan of action with each member will be one of the most important features of turning your recruits into leaders. Not only will you be training them how to do this for themselves, you are also demonstrating a successful and easy-to-duplicate system. Go the extra mile and never rely solely on your company's corporate office to train your new recruits. Do you find that you sit back and wait for your new recruit to call with questions? She may not because she doesn't know what she doesn't know! Become a part of her support system from the beginning and speak to her on a regular basis. Remember, success is made up of small, steady actions and you want her to experience success while she is still on her emotional high.

Transition from Trainer to Coach

Once your recruit has learned the basics of your company and business, it is time to implement coaching. Sometimes your new team member will approach you with a question that you may be inclined to quickly answer. However, it will be more beneficial to her if you let her find the answer. A common request for help is in the arena of sponsoring. Instead of telling her how you recruit or that she should mention joining the company three times during her show, try asking questions:

- *How are you inviting people to your show or presentation?*
- *What are your first ten words when inviting?*
- *What traits are you looking for in a prospect?*

Asking questions will transition your teaching style from training to coaching.

Coaching inspires action based upon asking questions, helping her discover the answers herself. It is not your job to provide all the answers. Instead of developing a leader, this will foster dependency. Part of successful coaching is guiding your teammate through self-discovery, being responsible for her choices and actions. As a leader, your function is to empower everyone on your team to become self-reliant, not dependent. You want to empower—not enable.

Oftentimes, leaders are relieved to learn that they do not have to have all the answers. It has much more impact when your recruit discovers the answers herself and by doing so, it is easier for her to remember the information and act upon it. It is also important to realize that your team members really *do* have the answers. They are often so close to the circumstances that their vision is sometimes clouded. Coaching your teammate during these times will offer her clarity and empowerment.

True success comes from learning how to serve rather than convince. This shift in how you communicate with your recruit will empower her to feel more confident and be in control of her own destiny. Not only will this help with retention, but also your team will move forward faster and achieve greater results.

A wonderful way to incorporate coaching is through a weekly coaching partnership with your recruit. Discuss what she accomplished the previous week and applaud her successes. Based upon her goals, discuss what she wants to accomplish the following week. Ask permission to hold her accountable to her goals. At the end of each call, let her determine her action steps to complete before the next call, encouraging her to incorporate a stretch into each step. You can touch base with quick calls throughout the week, offering encouragement and motivation.

Coaching is an intricate skill to learn. It will be difficult at first not to provide the solution. It is tempting to immediately respond and provide all the answers. However, this will not help her on her way to leadership. Create a new habit for yourself of pausing when a team member calls with a challenge. Respond by offering acknowledgement and asking questions, instead of telling her how to solve the problem. Continue to develop and hone this skill and there is no doubt you will see a difference in the success of your team.

Transform through Motivation

Consistent motivation is a key factor in the success of a direct seller. Positive feedback is crucial to keeping your team motivated and able to thrive, resulting in consultants who feel valued and confident in their skills. How would your team rate you if asked how well you motivate and inspire them?

Your company's corporate office has devised an incentive program that is intended to motivate the majority of consultants. However, not all are motivated equally. Each has a different set of wants and needs which will not always coincide with the incentive plans or goals put in place by the company. Through thousands of scientific studies on human motivation, we have discovered some very important information:

The two most powerful positive reinforcements for direct sellers are achievement and the recognition of that achievement.

So, first, you must help your recruits achieve success. Whether it is booking their first party or having their first $1000 show, you must help them create their goals and achieve those goals. Then, as they achieve those goals, recognize those achievements in ways that most motivate each individual.

Acknowledge through Recognition

Your first goal with any new recruit is to help her to accomplish something. Without achievement there is no positive behavior to reinforce with recognition. Keep her focused on her goals through your daily interaction and coaching. Then recognize each level of achievement that gets her closer to those goals—no matter how small. Recognition is one of the key ingredients to developing a new leader.

One of the major reasons that so many love this industry is the fulfillment they receive from acknowledgement. Recognize everything you can. Each small achievement is a small step to bigger and better accomplishments. Encouragement and recognition motivate people to reach new heights. Starting a new business can be scary, and everyone comes from different backgrounds. Therefore, everyone will progress at different rates. As they become more self-confident, their accomplishments will become larger and many will progress faster once they have passed the—sometimes overwhelming—

start-up phase. Recognition in front of peers can have an infinitely positive impact on the attitude and performance of your team. Never underestimate the power of recognition. Remember, what is recognized is repeated, so make sure that you are reinforcing the habits you want to develop.

Do look first at what your company already has in place in terms of recognition tools. Then consider what you might want to do in addition, especially to reinforce the simple and important action steps that are necessary to build a direct selling business.

One economical option is to purchase charm holders or bracelets that will hold four to six charms. Award charms that represent the beginning behavior you would like to reinforce. Examples could be a number five charm to represent five calls per day, or a star for signing her first recruit. Soon you will have the respect of a high-performing team of professionals who are growing personally and professionally because you had the discipline to find out what they wanted, helped them achieve it and recognized that achievement.

Persevere with a Positive Attitude

Direct selling is an emotional business. People buy into the business on an emotional high and they buy out of the business on an emotional low. Life is good while sales are up, but as with any profession, your recruits can get frustrated and discouraged. Sometimes, when a new recruit asks for a booking, the customer will say no. That's not so bad, but when she gets five in a row, she may get discouraged. Add a cancellation on top of that and your newbie may start thinking this is a sign. It is up to you to teach your team how to manage disappointment. Remember, most attrition occurs within the first 90 days.

What the dropouts fail to realize is that everyone in the business feels negative emotions from time to time. Successful people aren't immune to negative feelings, they have just learned to manage their feelings rather than let their feelings manage them. When successful people hit a low, they don't drop out. They persevere in the face of adversity, recognizing that low periods do not last forever. The three most common negative feelings your people will experience are disappointment, anger and depression.

This is the time to steer them back to their emotional "why" and do some coaching. First, identify the problem by asking her what has happened to cause her negative feelings. Then ask coaching questions, such as:

- *Do you feel like a failure?*
- *Does failing at something you do make you a failure as a person?*
- *Can you think of anyone who has never failed at anything?*

If you incorporate this lesson into the process of growing your new recruits, not only will you have more retention, but you will also have more leaders.

Pay consistent attention to your team. Don't wait until the end of the month when you are trying to finish out a contest. Notice their incremental gains and celebrate their successes. Additionally, when consultants feel connected to the team, they will be more likely to stay the course during tough times. Your team becomes a community whose members support each other.

Empower by Example

If you want a highly motivated team, *you* must set the example. You must demonstrate enthusiasm, energy, team cooperation, honesty, integrity and commitment. Treat people with respect and dignity. Give them the tools to excel, grow and develop. Encourage them to participate and get involved. Solicit feedback, listen to their comments, and act on suggestions that will help your business succeed. Set and communicate high standards, and provide positive reinforcement when your team members perform.

By example isn't another way to teach, it is the only way to teach. As your team grows, as a group and individually, they will have learned your duplicatable system. Subsequently, they will implement your leadership skills with their own teams.

Determine Your Destiny—Start Today

Imagine how your new recruit will feel as she starts her business with these new strategies in place. Imagine how much easier it will be for her to achieve her goals with the clarity of purpose provided by your new approach. What will it mean for you to have a reputation of producing leaders?

Commit to incorporating these simple techniques into your business today. Whether you create your new plan all at once or incorporate one strategy per week for the next two months, you will definitely see results. In the end, leaders are measured by results. After all, the true function of leadership is to produce more leaders!

SALLIE MESHELL
Destiny By Design

The "Dr. Phil" of direct selling

(318) 670-7444
sallie@destinybydesign.net
www.destinybydesign.net

With fifteen years in direct sales, Sallie has done it all. After years as a top consultant, she eventually started her own direct sales business and recently sold it—a happy ending to her own success story. Sallie's background includes credentialing from the Coaches Training Institute and a BS in Marketing from Louisiana State University. Drawing on her experiences as a consultant and business owner, she can address the challenges of this industry from all angles.

Sallie shares her passion and proven formula for empowering direct sellers to achieve the profits they desire. Personable and professional, she is respected in the industry and in demand as a speaker, trainer and coach. Having studied with Jack Canfield, her interactive workshops engage audiences as she integrates teachings on the Law of Attraction.

Informative and fun, Sallie reveals the secrets of determining your dreams and your personalized plan to achieve them. She helps clients transform wishes into reality by creating their own "Destiny By Design"—a blueprint for success to put you on the fast track leading to your goals, the bank and beyond!

More Direct Selling Power

Now that you have learned many things about how to build and manage your direct selling business, the next step is to take action. Get started applying what you have learned in the pages of this book. We want you to know that we are here to help you meet your professional and personal objectives.

Below is a list of where we are geographically located. Regardless of where our companies are located, many of us provide a variety of services over the phone or through webinars, and we welcome the opportunity to travel to your location to provide an in-person training. You can find out more about each of us by reading our bios at the end of our chapters, or by visiting our websites, listed below.

If you are looking for one-on-one coaching or group training, many of the co-authors in this book are available to support you. Feel free to call us and let us know you have read our book and let us know how to best serve you.

United States

Arizona

Tammy Stanley   www.tammystanley.com

California

Kimberley Borgens, CBC   www.bealegacy.com
Karen Clark   www.mybusinesspresence.com
Rhonda Johnson   www.makingtaxagame.com
Caterina Rando, MA, MCC   www.directsalescoaching.com
Cindy Sakai, MA, CDC   www.think-training.com

Colorado

Beth Jones-Schall   www.spiritofsuccess.com

Georgia

Lorna Rasmussen   www.absolutebestway.com

Hawaii

Gale Bates   www.mymentorbiz.com
Nicki Keohohou   www.dswa.org

Illinois

Martha Staley, CDC   www.yourperfectworld.net
                                                   www.marthastaley.net

New Hampshire

Lyn-Dee Eldridge, CPC, CPMC   www.lyn-dee.com

Ohio

Mary McLoughlin   www.marymcloughlin.com

South Dakota
Anne Nelson   www.yourjoyzone.com

Texas
Sallie Meshell   www.destinybydesign.net

Virginia
Marcy Stahl   www.marcystahl.com

Washington
Shannon Bruce, CPCC, PCC, CPT   www.yourgreaterpurpose.com
                                                 www.shannonbruce.com
Shari Hudspeth   www.averagetoexcellence.com

Wisconsin
Ruth Fuersten   www.booksellrecruit.com

Australia

Sydney
Gale Bates   www.mymentorbiz.com

Tasmania
Celine Egan   www.tcy.com.au
                                                 www.acceleratewomen.com

*Power*Dynamics
PUBLISHING

PowerDynamics Publishing develops books for experts who speak and want to share their knowledge with more and more people.

We know getting a book written and published is a huge project. We provide the resources, know-how and an experienced team to put a quality, informative book in the hands of our co-authors quickly and affordably. We provide books, in which our co-authors are proud to be included, that serve to enhance their business missions.

You can find out more about our projects at
www.powerdynamicspub.com

Also from
PowerDynamics Publishing

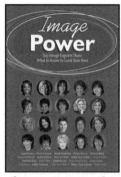

For more information on this book, visit
www.imagepowerbook.com

For more information on this book, visit
www.executiveimagebook.com

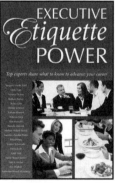

For more information on this book, visit
www.execetiquette.com

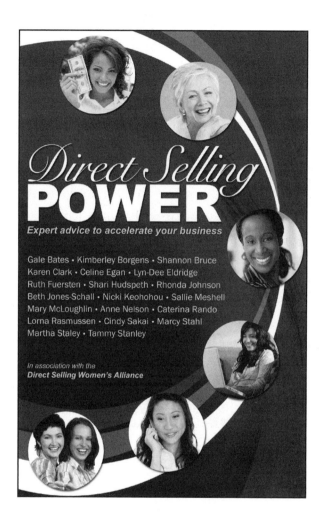

For more copies of *Direct Selling Power,*
contact any of the co-authors or visit
www.directsellingbook.com or **www.dswa.org**

For more information on any of these books, visit
www.powerdynamicspub.com

About the Direct Selling Women's Alliance

The Direct Selling Women's Alliance began around a typical kitchen table when a group of women shared the vision of providing an opportunity for others to live their lives more fully while balancing their personal and professional needs. Never, in the 100+ year history of the direct selling profession, had there been an association dedicated to the needs of independent network marketers and party plan professionals. Entrepreneurs from around the world now have a place to call their own: an alliance designed with their success in mind, an alliance to support the direct selling profession.

The DSWA provides a resource-rich website and cutting-edge virtual training courses specifically designed for direct sellers. We enrich the industry by providing personal and professional training through live and archived teleclasses, a learning library, collaborative leadership retreats, live events and so much more. The DSWA also offers extensive benefits geared toward making life easier, such as options for health care, discounts on office supplies, free e-books, and local chapter meetings.

We are excited to say that what began with a kitchen table discussion has grown into an international association boasting members from around the globe. The processional effect of touching women's lives has overflowed into direct selling companies, across gender and race, and into the next generation. One example of this phenomenal momentum is the *Build It BIG* and *More Build It BIG* books, which reached the top positions on multiple bestseller lists and featured outstanding leaders.

Yet another result of the growth of DSWA is The DSWA Global Foundation (DSWAGlobalFoundation.org), which offers scholarships to those wishing to enter the direct selling profession and to children of direct sellers. The Foundation also provides educational seminars at high schools, colleges and employment services throughout North America.

If you've been inspired to take more control over your life, then we invite you to visit the Direct Selling Women's Alliance! For more information on DSWA, go to www.dswa.org.

Inspired Style

Incredible Life

Get Organized Today

Incredible Business

...and more!